D1216791

Front cover :
Picture of dad (w/helmet on) probably taken in October 1969 sometime around his nineteenth birthday.

The blond-haired soldier at his left was from Louisiana. He also survived the war.

The young soldier squatting between them was from New York State. He was killed in action in mid-1970. He is still missed by all who served with him.

About a dozen young men were killed in dad's company during the year he was in Viet Nam. They are all still missed by those who served with them.

No one knows for sure how many young men in his company were wounded. The most common estimates thrown around at his company reunion's put the number of wounded in action at about seventy-five to eighty-five.

That would put the total casualty rate in dad's company at about 140% of it's "field" strength.

To
my FRIEND
BRUCE,

FROM
Ri

ANGELS ON OUR SHOULDERS

How I Earned My College Tuition Money

RICHARD WRIGHT

authorHOUSE®

AuthorHouse™
1663 Liberty Drive, Suite 200
Bloomington, IN 47403
www.authorhouse.com
Phone: 1-800-839-8640

© 2010 Richard Wright. All rights reserved.

*No part of this book may be reproduced, stored in
a retrieval system, or transmitted by any means
without the written permission of the author.*

First published by AuthorHouse 3/19/2010

ISBN: 978-1-4490-3027-8 (e)
ISBN: 978-1-4490-3026-1 (sc)

Printed in the United States of America
Bloomington, Indiana

This book is printed on acid-free paper.

CONTENTS

This book is dedicated to our father. The stories in it are his. It is also dedicated to all the soldiers he fought beside. This is their story as well. We are thankful that neither of us had to go through such a thing as war. We also pray that none of our children will have to experience what these brave young men endured. They have truly lived through Hell. Some of them paid the ultimate price. Many others were left disfigured or paralyzed, or both. Almost all were left with serious mental scars.

PRELUDE TO WAR

As the civilian airplane that I traveled to Viet Nam in touched down on the runway at the Bein Hoa airport (near Saigon), I remember feeling the sense of dread that swept over me. I had just recently completed training at Fort Polk, Louisiana's famous 'Tiger Land" school of infantry. It was expressly designed to prepare soldiers for combat duty in Viet Nam. There had been little doubt for the past few months as to where I was going to end up and what I was going to be doing when I got there. I had ended up in the Army's "bottom of the barrel", so to speak. I had been trained as a combat soldier and was about to experience a special kind of Hell that only combat infantry soldiers can be "sentenced" to.

I remember very distinctly the blast of heat that swept over us when the stewardess opened the rear door of the airplane. It felt like someone had opened the door on a blast furnace! God, it was hot in Viet Nam. I had landed about eleven degrees from the Equator and it was hotter and more humid than anything I had ever experienced before.

After debarking and "queuing" up into the usual military type formation we were loaded into green colored school buses. The buses took us to the replacement center at the huge Long Ben military complex. There was no glass in the windows of the buses. The openings were covered by a strong metal "chicken-wire" type fencing. We were told that it was there to keep people from throwing hand grenades in through the windows.

I don't remember how long the bus ride was but I do remember spending about two days at the replacement center before getting my orders assigning me to the 9th Infantry Division in Viet Nam's Mekong Delta region.

We didn't do much those two days that I remember. I got grabbed once and put on a detail to clean the rifles that belonged to the cadre at the replacement center. They were the old M-14 rifles like the ones I had trained with at Fort Leonard Wood, Missouri during basic training. Otherwise, I think we just pretty much loafed about, only being required to stand in formations two or three times a day. At each formation, the names of those who's orders had arrived were called. Those called then "fell out" of the formation, retrieved their duffle bags and marched off, never to be seen again.

I knew a lot of the guys around me, as our entire infantry training company from Fort Polk, Louisiana had been sent to Viet Nam as replacements for the combat units already fighting there. At the replacement center we were divided up and sent to various units. A group of about forty of us were assigned to the 9th division and were loaded into a two engine Army airplane for the ride to the 9th's base camp at Dong Tam.

We spent about three or four days at Dong Tam, doing a little last minute training while trying to acclimate ourselves to the ninety-five degree heat and ninety plus degree humidity. It felt like it was one hundred-ten in the shade! We were issued slightly used M-16's, given a brief chance to "zero" them in, and practiced war by going on some short night patrols. The patrol's were done in a "practice" area near the base camp that was relatively secure. Plenty of cadre with combat experience went with us to ensure our relative safety.

Soon enough our orders came down and we were assigned to various infantry company's within the division. Ten of us from my old training company were assigned to the same company down in the 2nd Brigade's Mobile Riverene Force. Four weeks later, when the 2nd Brigade was disbanded and we were reassigned to the 3rd Brigade, only four of us were still there to transfer. The others had all been wounded!

VERY LATE MAY OR EARLY JUNE

The first "Eagle Flight" (combat insertion into enemy territory by helicopter) I ever went on was the day I arrived at my new unit. They were preparing to go on a combat operation when I got there. I barely had time to get my field equipment issued before we left for the operation.

The supply sergeant issued me an extra canteen, grenades, ammunition, etc. Then my squad leader came over and hung a couple of one hundred round belts of machine gun ammo over my shoulders as well as a Claymore mine. He also attached a one hundred foot long rope to the back of my web gear. I felt like I could hardly stand up under the weight!

Then my squad leader informed me that I was to be the new "point man" for the platoon!

We were then shuttled via boat from my new "home" which, by the way, was a Navy troop ship. I was in the Mekong Delta and it was so inundated along the Mekong River that, in some places, base camps couldn't be built. Troops were quartered on these ships and got to return to them every three to five days for an overnight "drying out" period to help fight against the severe skin diseases like Tropical Immersion Foot (Trench Foot). Diseases like Trench Foot and Ringworms were a plague for the troops in the delta. While serving in the Mobile Riverine Force, I basically stayed wringing wet twenty-four hours a day.

Anyway, we were ferried right back to the base camp at Dong Tam, which I had just come from, and loaded into helicopters. The choppers lifted up and headed out. No one had told me anything about what to expect or about what was going to happen. I didn't know how many men were in my squad and I didn't even know my squad leader's name. I felt like I was a lamb being led to the slaughter, completely ignorant of my fate. I don't think anyone had even asked me my name.

After about a five or ten minute ride the choppers started to descend. I was setting at the open door of the "slick" with my feet hanging out and could see open fields ahead of us that were ringed by jungle.

As we were about to land a helicopter gun ship on the left of our chopper formation suddenly started to fire rockets into the jungle on the left. As the rockets started exploding, my heart started pounding from fear. Another gunship was above us and was also firing rockets into the jungle just ahead of our landing zone. A third gun ship on the right side of our formation was flying low right near the jungle fringe on that side and was pouring black smoke out of it's jet engine, apparently trying to provide a smoke screen on that side. All of the door gunners on the "slicks" we were riding in were also shooting their machine guns into the jungle as the choppers touched down. The noise from all the choppers, the exploding rockets and the machine guns going off all around me was incredible!

The choppers touched down and everyone got off quick, bending over low and running toward the nearest rice patty dike as the "slicks" roared away. All the door gunners on the "slicks" were hammering away at the wood line with their machine guns as they pulled up and away. The gun ships were making a second pass over the jungle and firing more rocket's into it as they passed by.

I looked to my squad leader and he motioned for me to get down and head for the paddy dike just in front of me. I guess I was probably overwhelmed by it all and was probably still standing upright and not moving very fast. I did as was told and got down behind the dike. Everyone around me was laying behind the dike in the water-filled rice paddy and they all looked really scared and nervous.

In a few moments the "slicks" were out of "earshot" and the gun ships had ceased to fire rockets into the jungle. All of the shooting had stopped! Not one enemy soldier was shooting at us! The LZ was "cold". I had just had the living daylights scared out of me and not one enemy soldier could be found! I thought that I had suddenly arrived at the real shooting war. As it turned out, this was just the "S.O.P." (standard operating procedure) used by this unit when inserting combat troops into hostile territory.

My squad leader had a brief conversation with the company commander over the radio, pointed toward the jungle in front of us and told me to head into it. I headed off toward the jungle, walking point. He told me to watch for booby-traps. That was the extent of my training to become a point man. Everything else that I was to learn about war I would learn as I went along.

I don't remember encountering any enemy soldiers that day.

June, 1969

The first time I was ever in a major "firefight", which is what G.I.'s refer to when speaking of an actual battle, was about ten days or so after I was first assigned to the 2nd Brigade's Mobile Riverene Force.

My company was being transported down a canal on three "Tango" boats. I don't know what the Navy's official designation for them is, but if you've ever watched a World War II movie, you've probably seen one. They're about forty feet or so long, have a relatively flat bottom and have a big ramp on the front that can be lowered to discharge the troops or a tank or whatever. John Wayne types always got out of them in movies like "The Longest Day" or "Saving Private Ryan" when they assaulted the beach. They were rectangular in shape, made from metal about one-eighth of an inch thick, and the front part of it had no top over the troop compartment unless the Navy guy's had rigged up a plastic tarp or something like that to keep the sun off our heads.

"Tango" boats were used extensively in the Mekong Delta to ferry troops up and down the thousands of canals that criss-crossed the flooded delta. There were no real roads in the delta as it was too muddy and inundated with water to build them. Rivers and canals were the road system in the Mekong Delta. Many of the smaller rivers and canals were effected by the ocean tides and actually raised and fell with the changing tide, leaving large "mud-flats" on either side of the rivers at low tide. The mud along the edges of the rivers was usually about three feet deep and was about the consistency of peanut butter. The canals had steep sides so they didn't have mud-flats. The heavy low-land type jungle just grew right up to the edges of the canals. Slogging through knee-deep mud was a daily occurrence in the Mekong Delta.

Anyway, my company was moving down one of the countless canals in three of these "Tango" boats. We had a couple of "Mike" boats along to give us protective fire if needed, but more about them later.

As we were moving slowly down this canal that couldn't have been more than forty yards wide, the VC/NVA suddenly ambushed us. They opened up on us from the left side of the bank with multiple automatic weapons and a couple of RPG launchers.

All of the guys in my platoon immediately dived for the "well" of the boat. The "well" was at the rear of the troop compartment and was the farthest below the water line of the boat, which still wasn't very far below the water line. Being new to combat, I followed their lead and dived into the pile of G.I.'s in the "well".

AK-47 rounds were punching little holes in the left side of the craft. Sometimes the bullets went all the way through it and out the other side, sometimes they glanced off the side of the boat and careened away. Sometimes they just went through the left side of the boat and ricocheted around the inside of the boat.

The Navy guy driving the boat full-throttled it quickly to try and get out of the "kill zone" of the ambush. Another Navy guy got up on the side of the boat to man the mounted twin fifty caliber machine guns. As the boat picked up speed the Navy guy on the twin fifty's began to pour fire into the left side of the canal where the enemy lay in ambush. He only managed to fire a few bursts from the machine gun's before being hit by an enemy bullet and falling down into the "well" of the boat amongst us Army guys already piled up there.

Our boat was up to full throttle and began to move out of the "kill zone" pretty rapidly. Bullets were still striking our craft, but we were getting away. The other two boats didn't fare quite as well. I was in the lead boat and we, therefore, didn't have quite as far to go to get out of the ambush "kill zone" as the other two boats did. We were pretty well clear of enemy fire within about thirty seconds or a minute at most. But, it sure seemed like it was a lot longer at the time! A lot of bullets had struck the little craft. I bet the "Tango" was hit at least fifty times.

The column of boats continued up the canal for a little way and then "beached" as well as possible on the bank opposite the one we were ambushed from. They picked a spot that had an open area nearby to aid in getting casualties evacuated by choppers. As the "Tango" boat that had been directly behind us began to off-load it's wounded, the real extent of the damage became apparent.

The boat I was in had only suffered from automatic weapons fire and, as I remember, the Navy guy was the only one on our boat that was wounded. The boat that was directly behind us had fared much worse. They had not only suffered from the automatic weapons fire but had taken a hit from an RPG rocket in the troop compartment as well. Shrapnel had ricocheted around the inside of the troop compartment and wounded several people. I don't remember how many were wounded, but I think it was about four or five. I know that a couple of badly wounded guys were put in the first "medivac" chopper and some others had to wait for a second chopper.

The third boat had apparently turned around or backed out of the ambush site as it was no longer with us, so I didn't know anything about it at the time. I heard later on that the platoon in it had suffered some casualties as well.

After evacuating our wounded, we were all loaded back on the "Tango" and it turned around in the canal to let us out on the enemy side of the river. As we off-loaded we could hear explosions coming from the area back down around the ambush site. Artillery was pounding that area.

The two platoons we had available formed into a column and headed out toward the ambush site. As a new man in the platoon, I had been assigned to walk point. I had little experience and knew next to nothing about the task at hand. I headed off into the jungle, praying that I wouldn't get myself killed. I have always thought since that making new guys walk point was one of the stupidest things that my unit ever did.

As we closed in on the general area of the ambush site, I could smell the distinctive odor of burning napalm. The "Mike" boats that I referred to earlier had been working over the jungle ambush site after the artillery barrage. "Mike" boats were a traditionally shaped boat about thirty feet or so long. They usually had a couple of machine guns mounted on the rear deck and one of any of several different kinds of weaponry mounted on the front deck. Sometimes the weapon mounted on the front was a large flame thrower that, if I remember correctly, had two nozzles on it that enabled it to shoot on both sides of a river bank at once, if necessary.

Well, one of these "Mike" boats that had been escorting us had one of these flamethrowers mounted on it. We called them "Zippo's", named after the famous cigarette lighter. The "Mike" boat had been squirting flaming napalm all along the canal bank at the ambush site.

When we got up to a point near the ambush site, my platoon formed into a skirmish line and went closer, "reconning" by fire, that is, shooting up everything in front of you as you advance. "Reconning" by fire is a very common method to use when approaching a known or suspected enemy location.

After moving toward our immediate front for about fifty yards or so, everybody spraying full automatic weapons fire ahead of them, we ceased fire. Directly in front of us lay the former ambush site. The area was quite chewed up by artillery fire and the first fifty yards or so up from the canal bank was pretty well burnt up from the "Zippo's".

Both platoon's then commenced securing the area, which basically meant looking over the little battlefield to see what kinds of interesting things we could find. Of course, we had to be wary of booby-traps and there was always the possibility that a live enemy soldier or two might be around. But, it was an interesting sight indeed for an eighteen year old from Illinois farm country. This was my first glimpse of major carnage.

We pulled a body out of a bunker that must have been killed by concussion, as it had no major damage like arms or legs missing and was more or less intact. However, it more closely resembled a pile of bloody rags than a human form. It was as limp as a noodle when we pulled it out of the thick, strong mud bunker we found it in. I bet every bone in that poor guy's body was broken. We also found a body in the debris that was burnt black on the back of it, from the top of it's head to about it's hips. No doubt, the "Zippo" had gotten him. I didn't look to see if he had already been killed by something else before the "Zippo" got him. Never thought about it at the time. But, I do remember thinking that I would hate to die like that, being burnt to death.

Soon enough, we hooked up with our third platoon and began to move away from the ambush sight, weaving our way through the swampy low-land jungle, probably looking for any sign of the VC/NCA that had ambushed us. After a while we stopped for some reason or another. As one of the machine gunners in my platoon stooped over to set his machine gun down, he apparently sat it right down on a trip-wire attached to a booby-trapped hand grenade. He took the full force of the explosion right to his head and the front of his body. His assistant machine gunner was standing right next to him and was hit just about as bad, receiving multiple pieces of shrapnel all over the front of his body as well.

People began to holler for medics and some of us carefully started working our way toward them, now fearful of more booby-traps. When I got near enough to see, the medic was already bent over the machine gunner, who was lying on his back and moaning softly. He passed away about a minute later, as we watched silently. Another medic had also come forward and was looking at the other fellow. He was unconscious and badly wounded, but alive.

The medics quickly did what they could for the guy, applying some bandages and tourniquets', giving him some morphine, and starting a plasma drip. A "Medivac" chopper was called.

As it turned out, the nearest suitable open area to land a chopper in was only a few hundred yards away. We loaded our casualties on make-shift litters made of ponchos with four guys each grabbing a corner of the poncho, and set off as quickly as possible for the open area. It took us several minutes to get there and a chopper was "inbound" as we came upon the open area.

As I was still walking point, when I arrived at the open area I started out into the field a ways to get far enough away from the trees for a chopper to land. As if on queue, some asshole with an automatic weapon opened up on us. He was across the open area at the fringe of the jungle, about four hundred yards or so away. Those of us out in the open quickly retreated back into our wood line and established a "base of fire", shooting across the open field toward the snipers location.

However, time was of the essence, as we had a severely wounded man with us, so an artillery barrage was called in on the snipers location to try and either drive him off or kill him. The arty came over within a couple of minutes after we asked for it. About five of our one hundred five millimeter howitzers (five being a common number of guns in a battery of howitzers) fired about three salvos into the wood line . Apparently it worked, as we heard no more from the sniper.

When the chopper appeared overhead, we went out into the open area, "popped" a smoke grenade to identify our location, and prepared to "dust-off" our two friends. However, at some point during this little drama, the second man died. We put both bodies on the chopper.

Our column crossed that open field and went to see if any trace could be found of the sniper. No trace was ever found. I have always hoped that the arty blew that little son-of-a-bitch to shreds. I doubt that happened though or we would have probably found him. He may well have been the one that set that booby-trap. His delaying our evacuation of the wounded man may have cost him his life as well.

Copy of the Mobile Riverine Assault Force After Action Report. The date of this action was June 11th, 1969. Dad's account is pretty close after forty years!

3 65 and XS 884 355) at 0740. The RAC then withdrew, and later returned to establish blocking stations along with PBR's on the north and south side of the eastern end of the island, as U.S. army and ARVN troops began a sweep of the operating area. An additional company and a LRRP (Long Range Reconnaissance Patrol) were also airlifted in the area. Only six sampans were searched with negative results a RAC on the northern side of the island secured the operation at 0600 on 4 June, the RAC in blocking positions on the southern side departed at 1800. PBR's continued in blocking stations until 5 June. Overall results of the operation were disappointing in that only 5 detainees were apprehended. The indication was that the VC anticipated the operation and departed the area prior to the establishment of the waterblocks.

Until the 10th of the month only two ENIFF's against RAC were recorded. Between 10-15 June however, 7 ENIFF's were encountered as RAC operated in various areas: The series began at 0830 as nine RAC were enroute to landing beaches on the Ba Lai River in Kien Hoa Province with a company of the 3/47th Infantry Battalion embarked. At a position 4 miles northeast of Ben Tre (XS 565 358) units received two B-40 rockets, small arms and automatic weapons fire. All rockets missed and no casualties or damage resulted. Suppressive fire was laid in with unknown results.

Enclosure (5)
CONFIDENTIAL
****

CONFIDENTIAL
[DECLASSIFIED]

A series of operations entitled "Soft Shoes" began along the Cai Hap River in Vinh Binh Province on 11 June. This area had not been worked by the MRF for over six weeks. Several days of watermobile assault landings, infantry sweeps and interdiction operations were planned. On 11 June, 13 RAC, with two companies of the 3/60th Infantry embarked, proceeded along the Kinh Ma Cau toward landing beaches. At 0820 they were ambushed by heavy B-40 rocket, small arms and A/W fire from enemy positions within the dense foliage along the banks. One B-40 hit ATC 112-1 resulting in three U.S. Army wounded (minor). Fire was returned and suppressed. Three troop insertions were accomplished in the Soft Shoe area on 12 June and the 3/60th troops were extracted in late afternoon all without incident. In transit along the Ma Cau canal enroute to the MRB, one enemy B-40 was fired at the RAC from a position 10 miles southwest of Ben Tre (XS 417 166). The round penetrated the port bow of M-1 12-2 to the mortar pit wounding one Vietnamese sailor and causing flooding which was quickly brought under control. Three USN were slightly wounded due to friendly shrapnel in the ensuing suppressive fire. At 1905, this time on the Mo Cay River, 4 1/2 miles southwest of Ben Tre (XS 482 238) and within sight of the MRB, the transiting RAC were again fired on by one B-40 which missed. No damage or casualties resulted. Fire was returned and suppressed by RAC and the overhead Navy Command and Control helo.

TU 117.1.5, consisting of M-131-1, A-132-6 and R-132-1 were ambushed at 1540 on 11 June from the east bank of the Mo Cay River, one mile north of Mo Cay City (XS 468 220) enroute from the MRB to a Fire

Enclosure (5)
CONFIDENTIAL
****

CONFIDENTIAL
[DECLASSIFIED]

Support Base (FSB) to pick up troops. Two B-40's were fired ; one hit Monitor 131-1 on the port side forward below the waterline which caused moderate flooding. A-132-6 received the other rocket on the port side aft causing minor damage. The units returned and suppressed the fire with 20mm and 105mm howitzer fire. Eight sailors were wounded in the action, five requiring medevac. The units proceeded to the FSB to effect repairs.

Heavy casualties were sustained by MRF forces during an ENIFF which occurred at 0945 on 13 June on the Ben Tre River, four miles southeast of Ben Tre (XS 576 282). Nine RAC, with Bravo Company of the 3/47th Infantry Battalion embarked were enroute to a beaching site when they came under heavy B-40 rocket attack. Z-152-1 received four rocket hits, ATC 152-6 received two rocket hits and ATC 152-11 received one. Fire was returned and momentarily suppressed. The RAC were forced to reverse course in order to facilitate evacuation of casualties; as they turned around they again came under attack from the same location. The RAC proceeded toward a FSB while 26 of the wounded were medevaced by an Army dustoff helo and the Navy Command and Control helo. Total friendly casualties were four soldiers killed, and 22 soldiers and four Navymen wounded. At the FSB a company of the 3/47th replaced the decimated troops and returned to the ambush site. A company of the 3/60th was also airmobiled into the ambush area to conduct search and destroy operations which yielded no contact.

ENCLOSURE (5)
CONFIDENTIAL

*"Tango" boat ferrying troops across
the huge Mekong River*

COMMENTS ABOUT BEING SNIPED AT

Getting sniped at was a somewhat frequent occurrence. I refer to being sniped at as any type of fire we received short of actually being ambushed. Sometimes it was just a single VC/NVA with a rifle taking a couple of "pot-shots" at us. Sometimes it was a couple of enemy soldiers firing an automatic weapon at us or at the choppers we were landing in. The point is, if the enemy fired at us briefly, then quit shooting, we considered it to be nothing more than sniping. However, we still took it serious.

I think that most of these sniping encounters were the result of what the military calls an "incidental encounter". Basically, that means that the VC/NVA patrol was just out doing the same thing we were doing (looking for trouble) and accidentally spotted us. They took us under fire briefly just to make us "duck and cover" so they could get away. I think it also served to alert other enemy units in the area that G.I.'s were nearby.

Essentially, we encountered snipers in about three different ways.

The first, and most common, way we encountered snipers was when we were out patrolling and would be crossing an open area after coming out of the jungle. They generally just emptied the magazines in their rifles at the point element (the first three or four guys they saw) and then hauled their freight out of the area. These encounters usually happened at a distance of three hundred yards or more and they rarely hit anybody. It just scared the crap out of us and held us up for a few minutes. We would then set up a hasty firing line and briefly return fire. Sometimes, if the enemy was a little more persistent, we might get arty to throw a few rounds at them if they had nothing of greater importance going on at the moment. At any rate, after such a sniping incident, we could usually continue our patrol pretty quickly afterwards.

I suppose the second most common sniper encounters were when we were coming in to an LZ while on "Eagle Flights". Since I was involved in at least one hundred fifty such combat insertions, the VC/NVA had plenty of opportunities to "try their luck". Again, the enemy would usually just fire at the helicopters we were in as we were about to touch down on the LZ. As soon as the choppers cleared the immediate area after dropping us off, whoever was shooting at us usually ceased fire and disappeared. If they didn't quit shooting at us we called in artillery and plastered the wood line they were in. The choppers usually landed about one hundred fifty yards or so from the wood lines so that was about the distance from which we were fired at.

I was of the opinion that we were sniped at on "Eagle Flights" no more than about a dozen times. In talking with one of my old platoon leaders at a reunion, he was of the opinion that it happened a little more often than that. We always heard that choppers were a favorite target of the VC/NVA because a reward was offered to anyone that shot one down. I have no idea if there was any truth to it.

On rare occasions we would stumble upon a couple of VC/NVA while patrolling in the jungle. Like the first two types of encounters they were just brief exchanges of gun fire. The big difference was that we were almost on top of each other when it happened. A couple of people shooting at you from fifteen or twenty yards away doesn't just scare the "bejesus" out of you. At such point-blank range, it's easy to get shot. We would have to react quickly or get killed.

We had to "hit the dirt" fast and return fire immediately with no time to set up a firing line. The first couple of guys in the column (usually just the point man) had to handle the situation by their selves until they could crawl back a few feet to find some protection and allow a clear field of fire for other G.I.'s behind them to be able to add their firepower. Such encounters could be very deadly!

I was hitching a ride in a jeep once, going to the brigade base camp to have a minor wound X-rayed. We were driving along on some little dirt road and "snap", "snap", a couple of shots went by us that were fired from a wood line a couple of hundred yards away. The driver just kept going. He said it happened along that stretch of road every once in a while.

I figured it was just some part-time VC guerilla that probably lived somewhere close by and the guy's hobby was "pot-shoting" at passing American vehicles.

Daily life in the Mobile Riverene Force

Sunday was no different from Wednesday. Days of the week were meaningless. The only holiday we ever observed was Christmas. The U.S. military called a truce that day.

Most of the time I spent with the MRF revolved around a never-ending three day cycle.

On day one we left the troop ship immediately after breakfast. "Tango" boats usually ferried us to the shore of some river or canal to begin the task of patrolling as a company-sized unit. Unless we made contact with an enemy force we patrolled all day long through fair-sized stretches of jungle, stopping only briefly to gulp down some cold c-rations around noon.

Since we left the troop ship with two quarts of water and four c-ration meals we received no re-supply chopper at the end of day one unless contact with enemy forces necessitated a replenishment of ammunition.

It got dark early in the jungle (sunset in Viet Nam was at about six-thirty PM), so about five thirty we "circled our wagons". The company set up a circular defense for the night, called an NDP (night defensive position). The nine squads in the company each posted a rotation of guards all night long. Everybody ate another quick cold c-ration meal and each squad set out a Claymore mine before beginning guard shifts, which went on from six PM until six AM.

We were always very short-handed in the infantry squads. If we had six men in our squad, that meant each man pulled a two hour guard shift. If we had seven men, each guy pulled one hour and forty-five minutes on guard except the squad leader. He was always the senior man and always pulled the last guard shift. Therefore, if we had an odd number of men in the squad, his guard shift was only one and one-half hours long. In the rare event we had eight men, everybody was so "tickled" we didn't know what to do.

Day two was basically a repeat of day one.

We pulled up the Claymore's at first light (about six AM in the jungle), gulped down another cold c-ration meal and commenced patrolling activities by six-thirty AM.

Often, on day two, we would be picked up by choppers at some point in the day and inserted into a different area to "assault" a wood line, then patrol in the new area until about dark. On some occasions, "Tango" boats would pick us up and take us to a new location to continue our patrolling.

We also received a re-supply chopper around four PM on day two. It brought another three c-ration meals for each man and also dropped off plastic gallon jugs of water so we could refill our canteens. The chopper would return about a half-hour later to retrieve the jugs and anything else we might need to send back to the rear area.

After the re-supply chopper left, we moved out and went to our new NDP to spend the night. These NDP's were always in the jungle, not out in the open rice paddies. We didn't do many night ambushes in the Mobile Riverene Force. Don't ask me why, though, because I don't know.

On day three we did the same thing as before, patrolling until about mid-afternoon. Then the "Tango" boats met us at some river or canal and returned us to the troop ship for an overnight "drying out".

The only variation on the above schedule was that some-times the patrols lasted for five days instead of just three.

When we returned to the troop ship, we had to debark on a large, flat pontoon that was secured to one side of the ship. There were little huts for each platoon to store equip-ment in built on this big pontoon. We weren't allowed to bring weapons or explosives on board the ship, so our "tools of the trade" had to be left in the huts.

Before we could actually board the ship, each of us had to be sprayed down with a fire hose. We were so filthy and covered with mud from patrolling in swamps and through tidal "mud flats" that the Navy wouldn't let us aboard ship until they "hosed" us down.

Once aboard ship we got a hot dinner that night and a hot breakfast the next morning before we left again. The Navy did have great chow!

We slept in the troop compartments for the night. I hated the troop compartments. They were crowded. The canvas bunks were stacked about four high and took up the entire compartment. Except for little isles between the rows of bunks, there was no room for recreation at all.

Each troop compartment had shower facilities, when they worked, which was not often. Besides, the water used for bathing was pumped in from the muddy Mekong River and was so dirty we considered ourselves to be no better off after a shower than we were before. Therefore, most people just didn't bother to shower at all, even if the facilities did happen to be working.

Anyway, after a couple of hot meals and a single night of sleep in a bunk instead of on the ground, the cycle repeated itself.

Never even once during the month or so I spent in the MRF did the Army make any attempt to provide us with any kind of diversionary recreational activities. Not a movie, not even a commissary. The only PX we had access to was the small commissary aboard the Navy ship. We could buy cigarettes there. That was all. Alcohol was apparently not allowed on the ship.

Life in the Mobile Riverene Force was miserable as far as I was concerned.

JUNE, 1969

My company was patrolling in a single-file column in fairly heavy low-land jungle some where, I believe, in Kein Hoa province. I was walking point and still pretty much a new guy with only a few weeks of combat experience. We had just hit a faint trail, and I was intently watching the ground directly in front of me for booby-traps. The guy behind me was supposed to be looking up ahead to try and watch for trouble a little farther on. It was supposed to be a kind of two man effort. That was a big mistake on my part. I should have been watching not only everything at my feet but what was farther up ahead as well. Never depend on someone else when gambling with your life.

I had just passed through a half-abandoned coconut plantation (row after row of coconut trees with an irrigation ditch between each row) and was crossing a little one log bridge spanning a small canal when I heard an explosion directly behind me. I had missed a tripwire and four of us had walked over it before the fifth guy in my squad tripped it It hurt him bad too. He was the M-60 machine gunner and was carrying the '60 on his shoulder and had his right arm up, hanging over the end of the barrel, to balance it This left his underarm exposed and, of course, that's where one of the pieces of shrapnel hit him, severing a main artery. The guy in front of him, carrying the squad radio, was hit also. I know he was hit in the calf of one leg pretty bad, but I don't remember where else.

Of course, I didn't know exactly what had just happened, I just knew there had been an explosion, so I jumped off the little log bridge and into the brush to my right This placed me ahead of my squad a little and separated from them by the canal. Within seconds, an automatic weapon, probably an AK-47, opened up on us about twenty-five yards away, directly to my front I can still remember hearing my squad leader yell at me to stay put. However, just seconds after he hollered at me, a second automatic weapon, ahead of me and to my left, also opened up. I felt alone and exposed with only some brush to protect me. I know that I shouldn't have done it, but I said to myself, "fuck this", and jumped up, ran back across the bridge, sprinted the twenty or so yards back to my squad, and dived into an irrigation ditch where my squad leader and M-79 man were both blasting away at the enemy. I ran directly into their line of fire in doing this, and it's a wonder they didn't accidentally kill me, let alone my being killed by all the VC/NVA bullets that were cracking loudly all around me. God himself must have been watching over me.

Anyway, since my squad leader was laying full-auto M-16 fire into the woods ahead and the M-79 man was thumping forty millimeter H.E. (high explosive) rounds out as fast as he could shoot and reload, I figured I should do the same. After all, this was what they were paying me that big hundred and ten bucks a month for. I flipped the safety switch on my rifle to "full-grease", stuck my head up just enough to see where I was shooting, and started laying fire into the jungle ahead.

Behind us, the medic and some others were trying to drag the wounded guys back a little to at least get them into an irrigation ditch or something to protect not only the wounded but also the guys who were trying to help them what little they could. Our platoon leader was also busy back there directing this little show as best as he could, as I saw one of the other squads behind us moving off to the left, apparently attempting a flanking movement.

It wasn't but a couple of minutes later that I heard quite a bit of shooting over that way. The other squad soon reappeared. They were helping someone along as they passed nearby, so I knew somebody had gotten shot. He was still walking under his own power, though somebody was helping him along. Later I found that they had walked right past a camouflaged bunker to their left and the VC/NVA in that bunker had opened up on them at near point-blank range with an automatic weapon. It was a wonder that our guy didn't get hurt worse.

The three of us in the ditch were keeping up a steady volume of fire, and were by now getting some help from another squad that was coming up on line with us. Their M-60 machine gun, M-79 grenade launcher and a couple more rifles added substantially to the base of fire we were trying to establish. Bursts of bullets from enemy automatic weapons fire continued to "snap" by over our heads.

Before long, another squad from a different platoon in our company joined the fray. They appeared about forty yards or so off our right flank and began to advance a little, crouching very low as they went. They didn't get far though, before we started hearing a tremendous amount of automatic weapons fire, both ours and the enemies. It sounded like the squad from that other platoon had hit a "hornets nest".

It was now becoming apparent what had happened. I had stumbled right into a small VC/NVA base camp area, complete with some bunkers around it to fight from. The booby-trap must have been their early warning system, and I had walked right over it and almost up to one of their bunkers before the other guy had tripped it and alerted them.

It wasn't long before I could see the guys from the other platoon pulling back. I don't remember if they had taken any casualties or not, but I don't think they did. If not, they were as lucky as I had been earlier. They had spent the past few minutes in a terrific shoot-out.

Right after that squad returned to our positions, we were ordered to withdraw, which was fine with me! Just as we were pulling back, I saw a loch (a small chopper, used primarily for observation) flying about just above the tree tops over the enemy positions. I could hear the VC/NVA shooting at it.

Shortly thereafter, I got a little surprise. I saw a propeller- driven airplane zoom over the enemy position as well. I didn't know the American Army still used them. Later on I was told that it was probably a South Vietnamese piloting it. The South Vietnamese Army apparently had a few squadrons of them. Whatever the case, he was flying very low and appeared to be just above the tree-tops also.

We pulled back a couple of hundred yards to the other side of the coconut plantation and found a small clearing by a little creek, just big enough to land one chopper in. A "dust-off" was called in to pick up our wounded and a re-supply chopper was also requested as some of us were low on ammo. We were all probably due for a re-supply of c-rations and water anyway. We formed a semi-circular defensive position, "popped smoke" to identify our position as the choppers came in, and settled down to "lick our wounds" as we watched the "show" that the airplanes above us were about to put on.

As it was late in the afternoon there was only time for one air strike on the enemy. Those little prop-driven planes did a god job though, and I got to see my first air strike as they bombed up ahead of us a few hundred yards. We had to keep our heads down when they dropped their bombs, but we watched them dive down before ducking and watched them circling overhead after their bombs exploded.

One of the planes dropped bombs that made the earth beneath us tremble as they exploded and we could hear shrapnel hitting the trees in front of us. The other plane dropped napalm. We could see the black cloud of smoke rising above the enemy positions after the napalm burst into flames on the ground. Everybody cheered when the napalm went off.

When the great little air show was over we moved off to our left several hundred yards and set up our usual company sized all-around defensive position. Our common night defensive position was circular in nature, with each squad taking up positions about twenty-five yards apart.

While in the Mobile Riverene Force we didn't do many night ambush patrols. We tended to hide out in the jungle.

God, the jungle is dark at night. You literally cannot see your hand in front of your face. Often you can't even see your hand in front of your face when looking through the Starlight night vision 'scope. When pulling a guard shift at night in the jungle, you just sat there with your rifle across your lap, the "clacker" (detonating device) for the Claymore mine in one hand and the handset for the radio in the other hand. If you heard anything, you called it in on the radio and "blew" the Claymore.

Anyhow, after darkness settled in, a twin-engined airplane code-named "Spooky" came on station above the VC/NVA infested area and began working out. It's a truly incredible sight to watch one of them shooting their mini-guns. The mini-guns had about six barrels that rotated as they fired and were capable of shooting bullets at the rate of about three thousand rounds per minute. The airplane would fly in a circle above it's target area and pour fire down toward the ground. Given that only every fifth round in a belt of machine gun ammo is a tracer, the mini-guns shot so fast that it looked like someone was pointing a laser beam toward the ground. The gun fired so fast that it sounded more like a chain-saw than a machine gun.

Later on that night, after "Spooky" had retired and I had fallen asleep, I was suddenly and frightfully awakened by the sound of gunfire very close by. Several VC/NVA had walked right up into the middle of the squad position that was set up next to us on our left. We never knew if they did it on purpose or just by accident, and we never found out if the squad's guard had fallen asleep. We only knew that there was much wild gunfire right next to us and everybody over there was shooting every which direction. All we could do was grab our weapons and roll into the water-filled ditch right behind us (we were set up for the night in the coconut plantation, with irrigation ditches every ten yards or so).

There was much hollering, cursing and shooting for about thirty seconds. Then the shooting stopped and the yelling became cries for the medics. Things over to our left had become what the Army referred to as a "clusterfuck". No one knew what was going on. Officers were coming up from the inside of our little night defensive location, radiomen all over the company area were calling each other for a "sit-rep" (situation report), and medics were calling to anybody that could hear them for assistance with the wounded. Most of the forward squad positions were calling on their radios for permission to blow their Claymores or to fire out into the jungle in front of us.

What it all boiled down to was this; one KIA (killed in action) in the squad next to us as well as one WIA (wounded in action). The wounded guy was hurt pretty bad. There also ended up being one dead "gook" laying on the ground right in front or that squad's position.

They took the wounded guy back to the captain's command post, hooked up two ponchos to make a tent, and, using flashlights, tried to care for him as best they could. We could hear the poor guy moaning and groaning. This put us in a tight spot. Between all the shooting earlier and the noise coming from the wounded guy, every VC/NVA in the area would soon know exactly where we were if they didn't already have a good fix on our location. Noise equals death in the jungle, especially during a time of war.

It quickly became obvious that we were going to have to get a "dust-off" with a "basket" on it that could be lowered through the trees to put the wounded guy in. This meant that a chopper would have to hover right over our position in the middle of the night, probably with it's search light on. Such an operation would expose both us and the chopper to much potential danger.

It took some time and it took some doing but we finally got the chopper overhead by turning on a strobe-light so they could find us. Now mind you, it was the middle of the night, in the middle of the jungle and enemy soldiers were no doubt lurking around somewhere out there in the darkness. The chopper came overhead, lowered it's basket and picked the guy up. All without incident, much to our relief.

The next morning as soon as it got light enough to see, every squad blew their Claymores and had a "mad minute", firing every weapon we had into the jungle in front of us. We did this when we thought enemy soldiers might be lurking about, waiting for a chance to hit us. Then we "dusted-off" our KIA and headed back toward the enemy positions, everyone feeling pretty tense and worried about our immediate future. Once again, I was walking point. We could hear the artillery up ahead, "softening up" the enemy positions.

We tried to come at the enemy from a little farther to the right than where we had been in contact with them the day before, in an attempt to flank them. After a while I hit a faint trail going in the direction we wanted to go, so I turned left and followed it. I hadn't walked far on that trail, maybe four or five hundred yards, when I could just feel the hair on the back of my neck stand up. Right next to me, on my left, was a small clearing with a little garden growing in it. Right past the garden were two rice-straw "hooches".

Standing between the "hooches" were the first two live VC/NVA I had ever seen, not more than fifty yards away.

They both had their backs more or less turned toward me, but I was sure they were the enemy as both were holding AK-47's. They hadn't seen me yet, by some miracle, so I ducked down and motioned to my squad leader to take a look. He crawled up by me and brought with him the M-79 man and the two guys who had taken over on the radio and the machine gun.

On the squad leader's command all five of us opened up on those two "gooks". I fired off a quick couple of magazines and then we hauled ass out of there. I don't know if we got them or not, and we weren't about to stay around and find out if any more were close by. We informed the CO. (company commander) that the VC/NVA were definitely still in the area. The CO. ordered us to pull back a ways while he called in for more artillery support.

After the artillery barrage, another loch appeared overhead to scout out the situation. The loch didn't draw any fire so we were ordered to "sweep" through the area. We did as ordered and encountered no more enemy resistance, finding only two or three dead bodies and a couple of blood trails.

My squad was ordered to follow one of the blood trails. I had never done anything like this before so I knew nothing of the potential dangers. My squad leader became rather nervous about it though and explained to me that following blood trails was dangerous. We could easily walk into a trap. The wounded enemy soldier might decide to "go down fighting" and we might not see him until we were right on top of him before he opened up on us. Also, the enemy sometimes set up hasty ambushes along blood trails, knowing that G.I.'s often followed them. He also mentioned that booby-traps were often placed over blood trails.

We followed the blood trail a little ways and the undergrowth started becoming thicker and thicker. After about one hundred yards or so the squad leader called our lieutenant on the radio and told him we lost the blood trail. We hadn't really lost the blood trail, it's just that nobody in the squad thought that one dying or possibly already dead enemy soldier was worth getting ourselves killed for. We rejoined the company.

As the company searched the area about a ton of rice was found. We destroyed it by burning some of it and scattering the rest on the ground. Some of the guys found a few things worthy of souvenir status, like a weapon or some NVA canvas web gear like a pistol belt or a back pack.

One strange thing I did notice. Grenades were strewn everywhere on the ground around the encampment area. American grenades, Chinese-Communist grenades, and homemade grenades made out of things like Coke cans. We never really figured that one out. Maybe the VC/NVA had a grenade factory in production at their little base camp, I don't know.

We saw no more of the enemy that day. I guess most of them had exfiltrated out of the area or gone underground, hiding in little "spider-holes" that we couldn't find. We policed up the grenades, threw them in some of the old enemy bunkers, and blew them up by throwing our own live grenades in with them. Weapons that weren't wanted as souvenir's were carried away by choppers. Web gear, canteens and things like that were burned up also if no one wanted them as souvenir's. Then we moved out, continuing our task of patrolling through the jungle.

PART TWO

JUNE 28,1969

I was transferred to a different brigade in my division. President Nixon had earlier ordered the beginning of the drawdown of troops in Viet Nam. The 9th Infantry Division was the first to go home, sort of. Two brigades ceased to exist on paper, and one brigade stayed on, attached to the 25th Infantry Division.

What the Army did was let all the men who had ten or more months of service in Viet Nam go home. Those with less time, like me (I had been in Viet Nam about five weeks), got sent to the 3rd Brigade or transferred to another division.

My new unit operated differently. Instead of continuously pulling three to five day patrols with only about one "Eagle Flight" every three days or so, my new unit concentrated on night ambush patrols and went on about three "Eagle Flights" about once every four days. This turned out to be a lot of "Eagle Flights", and, the more of them you did, the more it got on your nerves.

Instead of functioning as an intact company, my new unit tended to break down into platoon and squad sized groups to facilitate more effective night ambushes. Even our "Eagle Flights" tended to be done with one platoon being moved by four choppers as opposed to eight choppers moving half of the company and taking two "lifts" to get everyone assembled.

DAILY LIFE IN THE 3RD BRIGADE

My daily life got a little better after I transferred to 3rd Brigade. We pulled a lot more "Eagle Flights" and I hated that, but at least I now had a real base camp that could be considered "rear area".

The little camp had a mess hall that served hot meals (when I was there to get them) and a little PX (commissary) that sold things like canned potato chips, candy bars and camera film as well as cigarettes. It also had a small "club" that sold beer to off-duty troops. It wasn't much but it did have a bartender and it did have beer.

Special services even provided the battalion with a movie projector. Sometimes they showed movies, using the side of a building for a movie screen. The movies were shown outdoors, rain or shine. We just wore our ponchos and sat in the rain to watch the movies.

Unfortunately, the movies were only shown at night and the "club" was only open during the evening. All of us infantry guys were usually out on a night ambush patrol so we didn't have as much access to them as did the non-combat personnel. However, I did get to see an occasional movie and I did get into the "club" once in a while.

Most importantly, there was a small village near our base camp and that meant we had access to civilian females. We were all young men and needed a service that only certain young women were willing to provide, for a charge. While stationed aboard the troop ship while in the MRF we had no chance to interact with Vietnamese females during our off-hours, and that created a lot of tension among the men.

Anyway, my life now more or less revolved around a four-day cycle. Again, Wednesday was no different from Sunday.

On day one, we ordinarily got trucked out of our little base camp about mid-afternoon. Upon arrival at our destination we would patrol toward our pre-arranged night location, stopping short of the assigned area just before dark.

Stopping short of our night ambush location served two purposes.

One, we could keep our night location under observation until after dark when we were ready to move out. This minimized the possibility of getting ourselves ambushed while we were moving into position. Few things were worse than getting shot up in the dark.

Two, we could eat a cold c-ration dinner if we had left the base camp before the chow hall began serving the evening meal.

After dark we moved out and set up our ambushes in the assigned locations, usually no more than half a mile from where we had been waiting earlier.

Assuming everything went according to plan, we vacated our night location as soon as it got light enough to see the following morning. We would patrol our way back to the nearest dirt road and be trucked back to the base camp, sometimes getting in early enough to get a hot breakfast.

Day two was usually a carbon copy of day one.

On the third morning, when we were picked up after the second night's ambush patrol, we got the rest of the day and the third night off, in preparation for the forth, and most difficult, day.

On the forth day we did "Eagle Flights" all day long.

After an early breakfast (for those who could eat - stomach's were often in "knots" prior to "Eagle Flights") on day four we were picked up by choppers to begin our hardest day.

Normally we made about three insertions on this day, sometimes four. We came in on choppers at tree-top level going ninety miles an hour and dropped into an open field somewhere, usually about one or two hundred yards from a wood line. A skirmish line would be formed and we "assaulted" into the jungle. Once we got inside the jungle we formed a single-file column and patrolled the area for a couple of hours.

The theory behind this was that military intelligence (oxymoron) thought these areas likely to have enemy troop concentrations in them. Thanks to God that they were usually wrong.

After searching one of these areas for a couple of hours we eventually moved out into an open area, queued up into groups of about five, and got picked up by choppers to repeat the process over again until being returned to our fire base late in the day. We usually made it back in time for a late chow call, unless we hit trouble during the day.

Our contact with the enemy while on "Eagle Flights" was sporadic at best. However, booby-traps were a constant plague inside these wood lines and we took a lot of casualties because of them. The VC/NVA knew we used this type of tactic to keep them off balance and they boobytrapped a lot of wood lines very heavily, knowing we would be out looking for them.

We rested again on the forth night in preparation for beginning the four day cycle again.

What I just described above was fairly typical but by no means constant. After every two or three cycles we would often spend a cycle remaining in the field for three days and not come back to the fire base at all until the evening of the third day. We just took extra c-rations with us when we left and got a re-supply chopper to drop us more the afternoon of the second day. We spent the daylight hours on "sweeps", which was a fancy word for patrol.

We also got shipped out to really small temporary fire bases for seven to ten days at a time about once every six weeks or so.

These temporary bases were really forlorn little outposts out in the middle of nowhere, usually in the Plain Of Reeds. Most of them were nothing more than a little flat spot of ground that sat up a foot or so above the water levels of the surrounding marshes and stagnant, abandoned rice paddies.

They had absolutely nothing on them. A platoon of soldiers at a time would be assigned to them. The entire platoon would leave these little bases every night to go on ambush patrols so there wasn't even anyone there to guard the place at night while we were gone. Therefore, we couldn't even stockpile any supplies.

Sometimes these little temporary places stayed up and running for a few months and eventually three artillery pieces and a couple of tents would appear on them, but that was about it. Maybe some industrious group of G.I.'s would build one or two small bunkers on them before they were closed down. There was never any mess tent or any other civilized convenience on them. It was strictly cold c-rations. There wasn't even any extra water to shave with.

Other than that, they just served as a place to sit and let the sun bake your brains out during the day.

Excerpts from "Vietnam Studies - Sharpening The Combat Edge". It is a Department Of The Army publication, written by Lt. General Julian Ewell and Maj. General Ira Hunt. The publication is a combat assessment of techniques used by the 9th Infantry Division during the Vietnam war.

The Theoretical Basis of the Constant Pressure Concept

The Constant Pressure Concept paid off in cold results; however, in retrospect, its real strength was that it largely disrupted a Communist concept of operations which had proven successful since the early days of the Indochinese War.

The classic method of operating for a Communist unit (North Vietnamese Army or Viet Cong) was to take refuge in a relatively secure base area and spend some weeks reorganizing, retraining, and replacing losses of men, materiel and supplies. During this period, it would carefully plan a set-piece attack on a government unit or objective and then execute the attack with the actual movement to the attack, the attack itself, and the withdrawal taking place in a short period of three or four nights or less. If the attack, due to this careful preparation or other reasons, was reasonably successful, the government strength and confidence dropped and the more confident enemy recycled the whole procedure.

With the Constant Pressure Concept, friendly units upset this enemy timetable. By means of constant reconnaissance, small engagements with enemy units and pressure on their bases, the Communists were no longer able to rest 25 days a month; they could not refit and retrain and eventually could not even plan new attacks very well, much less execute them.

This process is very difficult to measure in any finite way. However, as a rough estimate, if the friendly forces (all types) in an area can diminish the enemy about 5 percent a month and achieve a friendly-initiated to enemy-initiated contact ratio of 3 to 1, the friendlies have the initiative and the enemy slowly goes down hill. In this situation, pacification proceeds and compounds the enemy's difficulties by separating him from the people who had previously helped him (willingly or unwillingly) by furnishing recruits, food, labor, information, etc. The best performance ever seen to my knowledge was in Long An Province where in 1969 and 1970 the friendly forces were able, months on end, to weaken the enemy about 10 to 15 percent a month and achieve a contact ratio of about 6 to 1. This paralyzed and eventually almost disintegrated the enemy, even though the Cambodian sanctuaries were nearby. This military pressure, coupled with a dynamic and most effective pacification program led by Colonel Le Van Tu, a superb province chief, brought Long An from a highly contested to a relatively pacified area in about two years. This was the perfect strategy-excruciating direct military pressure coupled with strong pacification hitting the enemy from the rear. The Cambodian operation, by denying the enemy a secure base, was the *coup de grace*.

Thus, by adopting tactics which not only bled the enemy, but worked against his classic method of operating, one could make impressive gains. This approach, while very obvious in retrospect, was not clearly seen at the time and was arrived at by trial and error. It required a high degree of tactical skill by the regular units (U.S. or South Vietnamese). When coupled with a substantial increase in Regional Force and Popular Force units to maintain reasonable and continuous local territorial control and security, the Communists steadily lost ground.

Preparation of Landing Zones

It has been customary in Vietnam for some time to deliver heavy preparatory fires on the vegetation cover around a landing zone in order to reduce the amount of enemy fire at the choppers and at the troops. This practice was essential in some places, desirable in others, and questionable elsewhere. The preparation might involve gunships, tactical air, and artillery and took from five to fifteen minutes, depending on the amount considered necessary and the complexity of the fire plan. As our contacts began to drop in 1967 and 1968, we examined this practice critically. We finally judged that the enemy had very few .50 caliber machine guns in any case and intuitively guessed that the time used for the "prep" was alerting the enemy and allowing him to evade. So we cautiously experimented with airmobile operations without using preps. After finding we received very little fire, we changed the Standing Operating Procedure 180°. No preps were used unless the commander felt the situation demanded it. This worked well-we had to go back to standard preps only in one place-a very tough area where we had one whole lift shot up due to a sloppy light prep. Not only did the no-prep policy increase our element of surprise, but it saved artillery ammunition, air strikes, and gunships for more lucrative targets. The biggest bonus was to relieve the air cavalry gunships so they could work with their parent troop. The lift ship gunships initially overwatched the insertion so they could intervene if necessary. After some weeks, we noticed that the enemy was "leaking" out of the area as soon as the lift ships began to land. We then shifted the gunships to watch the outside rather than the inside of the insertion area. This not only cost the enemy casualties, but held them in place. As a result we had, over a period of months, essentially turned the landing zone preparation around.

Insertion Distance

The original approach in open delta terrain had been to land our assault helicopter lifts 600 to 1,000 meters from the objective in order to minimize the effect of direct fire on aircraft and infantry. This meant that it took the troops an appreciable time and physical effort to make their way through the rice paddies to the objective. After observing the low incidence of enemy .50 caliber machine guns, we cut the distance to 500 to 600 meters and observed no problems. After a few weeks, we reduced it to 300 meters (based on effective rifle fire and light machine gun range) and had few problems. This reduced the approach march time by two-thirds to one-half and increased surprise. By the combination of eliminating preps and reducing the standoff distance, we increased surprise and lessened troop fatigue. Later on in 1969 the 3d Brigade of the 9th Division in Long An reduced their standoff distance to as little as 15 meters. The enemy by that time had little but AK-47 rifles to work with. This short distance was ideal, as surprise was almost total and only one or two enemy could fire at a particular chopper. Usually, they elected to hide instead.

Discussion

July, 1969

The four choppers carrying the twenty some odd soldiers in our platoon were coming in to drop the platoon for the second insertion of the day. It was late morning, probably about 11 AM or perhaps 11:30. The platoon was working in an area known as the Plain Of Reeds. On maps it shows as a "Waste Land". Hundreds of years earlier it was a part of the Mekong Delta's productive "rice bowl" area. In 1969, it was just a vast expanse of unproductive, abandoned rice paddies perpetually inundated with boot-top to knee-deep stagnant water. The area was punctuated by rivers and canals which were lined on both sides by narrow strips of jungle. The paddies themselves were covered in reeds growing about knee to crotch high out of the stagnant water. Hence the name, Plain Of Reeds.

Spaced liberally throughout this unpopulated wasteland were little "islands" of dense jungle growth. Apparently these were the former sites of small villages, coconut plantations, rich landlord's estates, or whatever. They varied in size from as small as two or three city blocks to perhaps twice to three times that size. They were usually square or rectangular in shape, but not always. The one the platoon was about to land in front of was more or less L shaped.

The choppers landed parallel to the top stroke of the L, their line of flight going toward the top of the L, like this (L↑), the jungle "island" to the left of the choppers.

As the choppers came in for a landing, two or three VC/NVA were spotted just outside the wood line, out in the open. Then the enemy fire started. Bullets could be heard banging through the metal sides of the choppers as they briefly touched down to unload their human cargo.

The choppers quickly cleared the immediate area and the sound of enemy gunfire could be heard clearly. Bullets from multiple automatic weapons fire were "snapping" overhead and cutting the reeds around everybody.

The platoon was in deep trouble, caught "flat-footed", out in the open, in a cross-fire of automatic weapons.

To me, everything seemed to be chaos and confusion. Everyone was diving into the stagnant water to try and escape the lethal hail of bullets coming from the wood line about three hundred yards away. I dived into the water as well and laid there momentarily, not really knowing exactly where anybody else was. It seemed like every time I moved a little, the "snapping" sound of bullets flying over my head and cutting the reeds around me would increase. I thought at the time that maybe the VC/NVA were shooting at me whenever I disturbed the reeds around me when I moved.

Bullets were pretty much flying everywhere! It appeared that a couple of guys had been hit while actually exiting the choppers and even more had been hit while trying to move away from the choppers. We always tried to get away from the choppers as soon as we got off them. Everybody knew that a chopper was a large and inviting target for enemy gunners.

I heard one of our machine guns open up just in front of me a little ways and decided to risk moving a little. I felt very alone and exposed laying in the open paddy just keeping my head above water, so I crawled up a ways and found my squad's machine gunner behind a dike firing his weapon. I got behind the dike and started firing my weapon as well. However, it seemed like every time I stuck my rifle up over the dike to shoot, the bullets "snapping" around me would increase. Bullets were even striking the dike in front of me and kicking up chunks of dirt as they "skimmed" over the top of the dike. I felt like it was almost impossible to shoot due to the volume of fire coming out of the wood line. When I rolled onto my right side to get a magazine of ammo to replace the empty one in my rifle I could see tracer rounds flying about above me.

The platoon could do little except lay behind the nearest rice paddy dike and try to deliver some suppressive fire with out getting killed while trying to do so. G.I.'s stuck their rifles up over the top of the paddy dikes and sprayed automatic weapons fire toward the wood line without daring to stick their heads up to accurately aim their rifles.

Helicopter gun ships were called in to help. They came overhead and began shooting their rockets and firing their machine guns into the jungle area. VC/NVA tracer rounds from their machine guns could be seen streaking up toward the choppers.

Artillery fire was called for and soon the wood line was being bracketed by salvos of exploding artillery rounds. Still the enemy fire continued while we could basically only lay in the stagnant water and keep our heads down.

There were a lot of wounded guys and they needed medical care urgently. A medivac helicopter was called for but had to be "waved off" because the incoming fire was too intense to try and evacuate the wounded.

One of the guys was shot high up on his shoulder near where the neck joins the shoulder. Another was shot across the chest (as opposed to through the chest). The bullet had passed through his pectoral muscle, basically tearing his nipple off in the process. He was badly injured. Our platoon medic had been shot in the arm. Other wounded G.I.'s were around as well.

Some of the guys in the platoon also had some very "close calls". One G.I. had the helmet shot right off his head. Another had his cigarettes secured to his helmet and the package of cigarettes was shot in half.

Air support was requested and F-4 jets came on station overhead and began to drop their deadly cargo's of two hundred-fifty pound bombs. Each jet carried four such bombs and they made tremendous explosions when they hit the ground. The jets usually dropped at least two of the bombs at a time if not all four at once. The shrapnel from the bomb's "whizzed" overhead and the ground underneath us shook. If memory serves me, one soldier was badly injured from the debris being thrown by the bombs. I think the chunk of earth that fell on him broke his leg.

At some point in time, a small observation helicopter appeared overhead and began to flit about above the wood line, apparently looking for targets of opportunity. It was hit by enemy fire and had to crash land nearby. The pilot either broke his leg when the chopper crashed or was shot in the leg while flying above the wood line, I don't know which.

Somewhere during all of this, a platoon from another company came along to reinforce our beleaguered platoon. They arrived on large hover-craft's. These vehicles used large fans underneath them to give them enough lift to move along over water or land. Smaller versions of these are used in places like the Florida Everglades.

Some of the platoon's wounded were taken out to the hover-craft's to be moved away to a safer place where choppers could airlift them to Army hospitals for emergency treatment. As the wounded were being moved out to the hover-craft's, the crew's of the craft's mistook us for enemy troops and fired on us with their machine guns. Fortunately no one was hit, but that little drama was nearly a catastrophe. As if things weren't bad enough already!

Eventually, enough ordnance (bullets, bombs and artillery) was put into the jungle area that enemy fire diminished enough to call in another medivac "dust-off". The remaining wounded soldiers were loaded onto it and evacuated, but not without mishap, if memory serves me. I believe a soldier was shot in the leg or ankle while helping to load the wounded on the "dust-off" helicopter.

Later on, the platoon gathered up and "swept" into the wood line. The "sweep" was not without incident though, as someone in the wood line either fired an RPG rocket at us or threw a hand grenade at us or something, I don't remember exactly anymore.

The jungle "island" was a scene of wreckage and destruction when we finally entered it. Bomb and artillery craters were everywhere. Trees were broken or knocked down, the undergrowth was ripped up and destroyed or stripped of leaves, and most of the enemy emplacements were blown up.

Everyone poked around very carefully, wary of boobytraps or live enemy soldiers. A body count was taken and souvenirs were gathered. I don't remember how many bodies were found in the wood line but I do remember that a nine millimeter pistol was discovered among the wreckage as well as some AK-47's, some NVA belt buckles and many other little trophy's. There was also scoop-shovels full of spent brass in one place where a large machine gun had been firing at us.

The platoon stayed in the area for the night and set up an ambush position out in the old rice paddies near the previously contested wood line. Movement was heard at times during the night but no one saw anything. Apparently any enemy soldiers still in the area managed to either hide or ex-filtrate out during the night. Those of us that had made it through this long day just laid in the rain all night, shivering because we had no ponchos to cover up with.

That night I think I felt about like what a motherless child must feel like. I had only been in my new unit for a little over a week and barely knew any of the guys around me.

My future looked very bleak indeed. I knew then that if I was going to survive the Viet Nam war, I was going to have to shut out all thoughts of my past life and everything I had ever learned about a civilized society. Nothing that my parents or my school teachers ever taught me was going to be of any value whatsoever in Viet Nam.

I was undoubtedly in a special kind of Hell. The only rule was going to the "law of the jungle". Only the very lucky and the very strong were going to have any chance at all of survival.

Troops loading onto HU-1 (Huey) "Slicks" in preparation for a day of "Eagle Flights" Note the door gunner at the rear of the troop compartment and his machine gun sticking up in the air. Also note the soldier sitting on the floor of the troop compartment with his legs hanging out. It was common for a soldier on either side of the "Slick" to sit that way. The troop compartment was so small that two soldiers had to sit that way in order to fit five or six people in the troop compartment.

Another good picture of a "slick", this was taken during an "Eagle Flight" by one of Dad's friends. In fact, the guy riding in it with his legs almost hanging out the door may be Dad. The soldier has no helmet or head gear on and Dad lost a helmet once while on an "Eagle Flight".

Hover-craft in the Plain Of Reeds.

Over head view of the Plain Of Reeds, taken from a "Slick". Note the little "island's" of jungle, the foliage growing along the canal and the areas of dense jungle growth along the river. Also note the hundreds of craters made from artillery rounds and bombs. It has been said that the total tonnage of bombs dropped in Viet Nam exceeded the amount of bombs dropped in Europe during the entire Second World War. This was a common sight in Viet Nam. Also note the water filling the craters and the inundated area's quite visible at top of picture.

On being a sniper

A few days after the fire fight in the Plain Of Reeds, I ran into the sergeant that was in charge of the battalion's sniper program. At the time, the sniper platoon consisted of him and one other sniper! He was actively recruiting for snipers and sold me on the idea of becoming a sniper simply because I would get out of the "field" (combat duties) for eighteen days to attend the school.

This training would be conducted at the 25th division's huge base camp near Cu Chi. I would get daily showers, hot food three times a day, and real wooden barracks with beds in them to sleep on. That's why I went; no other reason. I would get eighteen glorious days out of the rainy season weather, out of the "bush" (jungle), and have a roof over my head every night. Cu chi also had a huge PX (commissary - cigarettes, candy, etc.).

I learned a lot at sniper school. I learned to use a 3x9 power Redfield "rangefinder" 'scope, and I learned that a Starlight 'scope could also be used at night to kill with. It not only amplified ambient light, it was a three power 'scope with windage and elevation adjustments. I also learned to shoot past three or four hundred yards, reaching out to six hundred and even one thousand yards.

I couldn't hit the thousand yard target, even with a 'scope. It was only the size of a human torso and barely visible to the naked eye at a thousand yards. Over fifty per cent of most classes washed out of sniper school. I was among that fifty per cent that failed. I just couldn't judge the windage good enough at that distance to hit the target, and it was necessary to hit it to graduate from the school.

Upon returning to my unit, the sniper platoon sergeant asked me what happened. I explained the situation and he asked me if I wanted the job anyway, as they were so short' handed. He told me mat I would still get all the "perks" like periodic trips back to Cu Chi to re-zero my rifle, less helicopter assaults, etc., so I agreed. He acquired a "National Match" M-14 for me, we marked off some targets, and I zeroed in the rifle, a Redfield 'scope, and the Starlight 'scope. Then I spent about the next six weeks as a battalion sniper.

Most of my time was spent going on night ambush patrols with various units in the battalion. I usually ended up with a platoon from Alpha or Delta companies but also worked with the reconnaissance platoon frequently. I guess the other sniper was either assigned to or preferred to be with Bravo and Charlie companies. At any rate, we never worked together.

However, I did end up going on more daylight patrols and "combat assaults" on the chopper's than I had hoped for.

As a sniper, my task was to simply take the first shot which was, in turn, the signal to "blow" the "bush". I rarely got a second shot. The Starlight 'scope was a light amplifying device and the muzzle flash of my rifle would briefly "blank out" the 'scope by overloading it's sensors with light. The VC/NVA rarely ever gave me a second chance to see them. Also, if other GI's were shooting right next to me, the 'scope would usually stay "blanked out" due to their muzzle flashes. But, by triggering the "bush" with a well-aimed first shot, we increased our chances of getting more kills, and that was the name of the game, kill as many as we could. I was credited with six kills during this six week period of time.

Most of my shots, though not all, were taken at seventy-five yards or less. Sometimes we would spot VC/NVA walking in the open that were too far away to "blow" a "bush" on (about fifty or seventy-five yards was the maximum range for triggering an ambush if any success was expected) and, on occasion, I would be allowed to try a shot. Most of the time I wasn't allowed to shoot though, as my shot would reveal the presence of our patrol, thus compromising our chances of actually "blowing" a "bush". Revealing our position could also be dangerous to us, as any VC/NVA in nearby wood lines could take us under fire in our exposed positions out in the open fields.

I would also like to mention at this time that my experiences as a sniper were nothing like that stuff you see on T.V. or read about in books. We didn't hide in trees and we didn't prowl about behind enemy lines for days at a time.

As far as I'm concerned, hiding in a tree is stupid. How in the world would I ever get away once I was spotted? As for being behind enemy lines by yourself for days at a time, how would you survive alone? Even those LRRP (long range reconnaissance patrol) guys and Special Forces guys went in with teams consisting of several guys.

Anyway, after about six weeks of this duty, our battalion commander got wind of the fact that an unqualified guy was pulling sniper duty, and basically fired me. I was re-assigned back to my old unit.

AUGUST, 1969

By August, though unqualified, I was working as a battalion sniper. I had hoped to avoid going on many "Eagle Flights" but it just didn't work out as I had hoped.

One day I was working with some platoon or another and we were doing "Eagle Flights". On one of our insertions, somewhere in the Plain Of Reeds I'm pretty sure, we received some sniper fire. I don't remember if it was while we were getting off the choppers or if it happened a few minutes later, while we were forming up our skirmish line in preparation for our "assault" into the wood line. Whatever the case, we all ended up on our bellies in the water and hiding behind a dike for a while. I don't believe anyone had gotten shot or anything like that.

A loch or a Cobra gun ship, one or the other, came overhead and "buzzed" about over the jungle to look around a little. I don't think it saw anything of value as I don't remember it firing any rockets or anything like that.

Anyway, we eventually skirmished our way up to the wood line. When we got there, we could see a couple of VC/NVA posted signs warning of booby-traps. This was something the VC did once in a while. Whether or not there were actually booby-traps was not always the point. These signs were a potent psychological tool to use on G.I.'s as well as a warning for any civilians in the area. As we were in or very near the Plain Of Reeds we knew there weren't many civilians around the area we were in.

We took these signs very seriously! The troopers I was working with did not want to go into the wood line, nor did I for that matter. However, this was our job so we formed a column and headed into the jungle to patrol around a while and see if we could find any sign of the enemy. Everybody was really nervous and had the "creeps". We all just knew something bad was going to happen.

The platoon hadn't gotten far at all when the point man tripped a booby-trap, injuring himself seriously. The guy that was walking behind him was also hit by some shrapnel if I remember correctly. As soon as the booby-trap went off, two or three automatic weapons opened up on the point element from near point-blank range and at least one guy got shot.

I was never so glad in my life as I was that day to be in the middle of the platoon with the CP (command) group. Due to my status as a sniper, I normally stayed with a platoon's lieutenant and his radio men while on daylight patrols.

Even so, we were caught in a serious ambush. There were plenty of rounds "snapping" by our heads and "clipping" the foliage around us.

Anyhow, everybody "hit the dirt". Most of us in the column were directly behind the point element in a more or less straight line, following the trail the point man was breaking as he went along. We could do little to help at the moment because it is way too dangerous for people to be trying to shoot over each other's heads. The squad on point duty was on their own momentarily.

The platoon leader, his radiomen and the medic began trying to work their way up a little closer to the front to try and get a better handle on the situation, leaving me with the platoon sergeant, if memory serves me. The platoon sergeant then got the platoon's other squad, which was behind us, to set up a firing line and be ready to provide suppressing fire as soon as we could get the guy's from the point squad extricated.

The firing up ahead soon slacked off considerably and men started appearing in front of us, crawling our way to get out of the kill zone. Unfortunately, one of the wounded guys couldn't be brought back. With two or three guys wounded, the other four or five guys in the point squad lacked the manpower to do what had to be done. They needed to lay down plenty of suppressive fire to cover the guys that would have to pull the wounded G.I. out of the kill zone.

The job of recovering the wounded guy then fell on the lieutenant, his radio men and the platoon's other squad that had been following along at the rear of the column. Since the enemy gun fire had died off considerably, we figured that, with a little luck and both of the platoon's machine guns providing suppressive fire, we could pull this off.

Some of the guys in the platoon's second, and only other, squad began working their way toward the wounded man while the machine gunners, some M-79 men and a few riflemen side-slipped to the left a little and began "hosing" down the area where we thought the "gooks" had been shooting from.

Before long, we heard another explosion just up ahead of us, closely followed by a lot of gun fire. Someone up ahead had tripped another booby-trap that had somehow been missed before and a couple of VC/NVA were still waiting around, knowing we would try and recover the wounded guy. The platoon's second squad ended up with a couple more wounded guys before the VC/NVA broke contact and slipped away.

We did recover our wounded personnel and got them back out into the rice paddies. A medivac "dust-off" picked them up (it may well have taken two "dust-off s", I don't remember) and took them away.

All the guys in the platoon were really "pissed". They had not wanted to go into that wood line and considered the "Tu Dia" (Danger Zone in English) signs to have been fair warning. They cussed the lieutenant, they cussed the captain, and they cussed the Army for sending them into what we all considered an obvious trap.

Afterwards we were forced to walk all the way back to our base camp which was several miles away. Apparently our lieutenant had told the captain how "steamed up" everybody was and they decided to let us "walk it off". If I remember correctly it was well after dark by the time we got back to camp. We had no c-rations with us and missed our dinner as well. That "pissed" us also.

An unusual afternoon

One day in August, or perhaps early September, the "Recon" unit I was attached to as a sniper for the day was laboring away at one of the countless patrols that we were always going on. We had just exited a patch of jungle and were walking along on the dikes in an open area full of rice paddies interspersed with the occasional farmer's one room rice straw "hooch".

We noticed a small "knot" of civilians gathering up ahead of us a few hundred yards. To survive in war, one must be ever vigilant. We kept a close eye on everything around us as we drew closer to the little group of locals gathered up ahead.

As we neared the small group of people, an older farmer started down the rice paddy dike we were approaching on and began saying "boxie" as he approached us. I don't know exactly what "boxie" means in Vietnamese, nor do I know how to correctly spell it. However, most G.I.'s in Viet Nam loosely interpreted it to mean "doctor", we knew the old guy was referring to our medic.

As it turned out, a young woman was about to give birth, and the "knot" of people around her turned out to be mostly a bunch of other women gathering to help her.

Our medic went over to the girl in labor while the dozen or so of us G.I.'s gathered around to watch. Being young men of eighteen, nineteen and twenty, and in forced bachelorhood, we were quite naturally curious about such going's on. The young lady seemed to take it all in stride, considering she had a large audience of horny young soldiers gaping at her. She basically ignored us and concentrated on the task at hand.

The pregnant girl was squatted down and a woman on either side of her was holding her by the arms. Some old clothes or rags or something like that was laying on the ground between her legs.

The whole scene was really pretty organized and quiet. We could hear the girl grunt or groan a little every once in a while but she also seemed to be carrying on an intermittent conversation with the other women around her. Since none of us G.I.'s could speak their language, we had no idea what they were talking about. It all seemed to look pretty routine for them.

The medic stood near the girl with his medical bag open and at the ready while the rest of us stood a barely respectful twenty feet or so away, just trying to see between the women gathered around the mother-to-be.

As the girl's labor intensified, a funny thing happened. The war in Viet Nam stopped for us! The little miracle that we were witnessing began to sink in on us.

For just a few minutes we all forgot that we were in the business of hunting down and killing the well armed enemy soldiers that were also trying to hunt us down and kill us. For just a few moments we ceased being both predator and prey. The weight of war momentarily lifted from our shoulders and the guys around me that rarely had anything to smile about started smiling rather sheepishly. The tropical heat that constantly smothered us lifted and became less intense and the weariness of body and soul dissipated, then disappeared. We became almost serene. I hadn't felt that good in quite a while!

For just a brief few minutes, a young Vietnamese mother-to-be had melted the hardness in our hearts and allowed us to feel human again instead of like predatory animals.

My thoughts drifted back to the civilized life I once led that had seemed so far away and forgotten, suppressed by the necessity of needing to focus so hard on the dangerous and difficult job of being a combat soldier. I could see in my mind the faces of my parents, my brothers and sisters, my old girlfriends and others. I could picture the house I grew up in and the street I lived on.

Suddenly all the women started talking excitedly and acting much more animated. I never saw the actual birth of the baby because of all the women blocking my view, but we all knew the girl had the baby. The medic was helping them do something, but I didn't see what that was either. I guess he was helping to tie off the umbilical cord or something.

The young mother then went into the "hooch". She was holding the baby in one arm and with her other hand she was holding a bandage between her legs. The medic had given her the bandage. I don't think she was hemorrhaging or anything like that, though. I think he had just given it to her in trying to be helpful. A couple of the women went into the "hooch" with her and the rest of the people headed for home or went back to whatever they were doing before the blessed event.

We all put our helmets back on, shook our heads to clear our thoughts, and went back to what we were doing. The weariness crept back upon us and the heat became oppressive again. We rejoined the war.

None of us ever spoke of the event afterwards. I never even learned the sex of the child. However, I'm sure everyone felt the same as me in the end; Much richer for the experience.

Sept 16, 1969

This story made national news! Our battalion command-er was killed in action. It was the result of an accidental mid-air collision between his command and control heli-copter and a Cobra gunship.

I don't remember if I was back in my old platoon or if I was still assigned to sniper duty and just happened to be working with my old unit. Whatever the case, it doesn't matter. I was basically just a bystander when the accident happened anyway.

The company was out on a routine daylight "sweep" (pa-trol) and the colonel was flying overhead in his C.C. "ship" to observe and direct the operation. Apparently he spotted some movement in a nearby wood line and called down to the platoon to have it checked out.

Three or four guys went over to the wood line to see what they could see. Why the whole platoon didn't go, I don't know. The platoon sergeant, a squad leader and maybe a radio operator and one other guy are the one's that went into the wood line. That's all I can remember.

Anyway, if I remember correctly, the C.C. ship came down low and someone in the chopper began shooting out of the pilot's side window or the side door with either a pistol or, more likely, an M-16 rifle.

By the time our guys entered the wood line, a Cobra gunship was also overhead. Both choppers were flying around over the wood line.

Gunfire broke out inside the wood line. The guys in there had run into something. The colonel's C.C. ship was pretty much directly over the guys inside the wood line and someone in the chopper was still firing down into the thick foliage where our guy's were.

As the C.C. ship pulled upward to make another pass, it ran directly into the Cobra helicopter. I think the Cobra was coming down at the time, probably to have a look at the action below. Whatever the case, the two helicopters collided in mid-air. The C.C. ship came up under the Cobra and, apparently, caused the collision by flying directly into the path of the Cobra.

The two choppers fell to earth. The Cobra sort of looked like it was riding "piggy-back" on top of the C.C. ship for a time. The two choppers hit the ground not far apart and began to burn furiously, aviation fuel spewing everywhere.

I guess it would be safe to say that I, and everyone else around, was "thunderstruck", the two pilots in the Cobra gunship were killed as were all of the occupants of the Command and Control helicopter. Our brigade commander also happened to be in the C.C. ship for whatever reason and was among those killed.

The platoon sergeant that had entered the wood line had also been killed by gunfire down in the jungle. He was shot in the head by enemy gunfire and died instantly. A squad leader that had gone into the jungle was also badly wounded in the same brief exchange of gunfire. He was hit twice in the left arm, once in the left shoulder, and once up high in the left side of his chest by a burst from an automatic weapon.

All in all, about twelve people were killed and one was wounded during this brief, though terrible, occurrence. That's a lot of people to be killed so suddenly.

All of a sudden, September 16th had become a long day! We had lost both our battalion and brigade commanders in the blink of an eye. A simple accident took out more high-ranking American soldiers than the VC/NVA could have ever hoped to take out even with careful planning and a dozen deliberate ambushes.

The "brass" (other officers and/or high ranking non-commissioned officers) came out to view the damage and talk to us. Everybody was pretty shook up!

The company eventually resumed it's sweep. Somewhere along the line another guy from the company hit a booby-trap, wounding himself badly. I don't remember anyone else being hit by the booby-trap.

The information on the following page was taken from a web-site. It can be found by bringing up ArmyAir-Crews.com. Dad was incorrect when he said twelve people were killed. Eleven people were killed. Ten from the choppers plus one soldier on the ground. The correct date was September 17th, not September 16th.

17 SEP 69
W01 Robert P. Mayer [AC]
1LT Richard A. Snowdon [CP]
SP5 William A. Fitch [CE]
SP5 Gary L. Haught [G]
CPT Donald W. Dietz
MAJ Dana W. Mitchell
LTC Leo P. Sikorski
MAJ David R. Mackey
MAJ William T. McNair
COL Dale J. Crittenberger
Long An Province
HHC 3 BDE
#67-17821
Mid-air with <u>AH-1 #68-15061</u> during mission.

NIGHT AMBUSH PATROLS

Night ambush patrols were the "meat and potatoes" of my unit's war in Viet Nam. We got a lot of kills this way and rarely took any casualties when we "blew" them. I was actively involved in "blowing" at least three dozen to three and one half dozen ambushes during my year in Viet Nam. No one I've talked to at the reunions knows exactly how many, we just know it was a lot. We probably got at least one kill about seventy-five percent of the time.

Since we did night "bushes" all the time, we got pretty good at it. I will try and describe a typical night ambush patrol.

When we arrived at our night location it was always, by necessity, after dark. If the squad leader was smart he would always set the machine gun up just to his left and put the radio man just to his right. This was the "nerve center" so to speak. He then had his machine gunner close at hand

and also had easy access to the radio. Communication was critical. At the very least we had to notify our lieutenant immediately prior to actually "blowing" the "bush" so he could make arrangements with arty or mortars to fire illumination rounds overhead as quickly as possible after we initiated contact. We needed to see what we were shooting at if at all possible.

When I was a squad leader I always insisted that a man with an M-79 grenade launcher was just to the right of the radio man. That gave me relatively immediate access to him if I needed to direct or re-direct his fire. That mostly depended upon how much experience that man had. The more experienced he was the less I had to worry about him. Newer guys tended to put their H.E. (high explosive) rounds either too close in, which would cause us to get hit by shrapnel, or too far out, which made them useless. I liked it best when the M-79 man put his first couple of rounds just behind the enemy, then started working his rounds off toward whichever direction the enemy was most likely to run away at. That way, we would catch the VC/NVA both in the "kill zone" and again as they were trying to get out of the "kill zone".

I always made sure the assistant machine gunner was just to the left of the machine gunner. He could fire his own rifle when we "blew" the "bush" if he wanted, but he needed to be right on top of things if the machine gunner had any trouble like a twisted belt of ammo or something like that. We always linked together most of our one hundred round belts of ammo each night so the machine gunner had easy access to most of the one thousand rounds that each squad carried as a minimum. This was just in case we needed it. Sometimes things didn't go exactly as planned. Not often, thank God, but sometimes. We were in a dangerous business to say the least. One screw-up could cost a lot of people their lives.

After I had the machine gun crew, the radio man and the M-79 man set up I didn't particularly care where the others set up, assuming I had any other men in the squad. We were always so short-handed. If I had enough personnel, the first extra man I had would be assigned a second M-79 and I preferred him to be just to the left of the machine gun team. I would put the more experienced M-79 man down there if I had two of them. Extra riflemen, if I had any, were assigned to hold down the ends of the firing line.

I was also particular, to the point of superstitious, about how I laid out my personal equipment. It was essential to know exactly where every piece of equipment you owned was if you were going to try and kill somebody in the middle of the night and not get yourself killed in the process.

I always folded my web gear in a certain way, so that any grenades I had would be right on top and easily accessible if I needed them. I didn't want them to get caught on anything if I needed to get them off the suspenders of my web gear.

Then I laid my ammo bandoleers right across my web gear, open ends facing me. I preferred to put my rifle magazines in bandoleers instead of those little pouches that held three magazines. Then I pulled a few of the magazines just a little ways out of the bandoleer pockets so I could get to them easily. But, I was always careful not to pull them out too far. That way they wouldn't fall out if I had the time to actually tie the bandoleers around my waist before we "blew" the "bush".

Time rarely permitted that though, as we usually had less than a minute to awaken everyone, establish a firing line, and radio in for illumination to fire at the platoon leaders command. We also needed to let as many people as time permitted look through the Starlight 'scope to help everyone establish a sense of distance from us to the enemy. That usually wasn't far though. Most of our ambushes were probably "blown" from between twenty and forty yards away. The Viet Nam war was, for me, a war that was routinely fought at point-blank or near point-blank range.

After all else was in order I laid my two or three parachute flares down just to the left of my web gear. I needed them handy because, as a squad leader, I had to see to it that we had illumination up immediately so we could see what we were shooting at. I didn't want to trust a new guy with such a responsibility.

The arty or mortars could not shoot their rounds until we actually started firing so it could take a minute or so before we had their large flares overhead. It took a while for their illumination rounds to travel the distance to our location. Sometimes we would be several miles from the nearest arty position and "flight" time alone could eat up several seconds. As stated above, we also had little or no "lead" time between spotting the enemy and "blowing" the "bush". The arty and mortar guys had to get to their weapons, get the proper direction and distance "dialed" in, and get the guns loaded before they could shoot. We often "sprang" the ambushes before the arty or mortars were ready. Therefore, the little parachute flares we carried with us were essential.

The little parachute flare is how I signaled the squad to "blow" the "bush". When they heard the flare go "sizzling" up into the air, everyone started shooting. Within about two seconds after commencing fire, the little parachute flare would open above us and give us enough light to help us see what we were shooting at until arty or mortars could get some "lum" overhead. As soon I hit the flare on the ground to set it off, I came up shooting also.

Shooting fast and accurate made the difference when triggering an ambush. We needed to get a volume of fire out but it needed to be accurately placed. I generally shot about the first two magazines on full-auto, using controlled two or three round bursts. Then I followed up with about three more magazines on semi-auto. I basically "swept" back and forth at the ground in front of me, widening my "kill zone" with each successive magazine of ammo.

If one of the VC/NVA we were shooting at was dumb enough to still be upright and running, we just shot at him until he went down. Usually, all we could see was their heads and knees sticking up just above the rice paddy dike that they were hiding behind as they ran to get out of the "kill zone".

Those guys could get down behind a dike no more than about a foot high and run like hell that way. It was incredible to see!. I can only describe it as a kind of a "duck-walk". They were so small and skinny they could run with their butts practically dragging the ground and only their heads and the tops of their knees showing above the dikes. And, I mean, they could move fast that way! Of course, I'm sure that hundreds of bullets flying about only inches from them was an excellent motivator.

Anyway, we would "sweep" out toward the "kill zone" afterwards under the light of the parachute flares. If we saw anyone lying out there as we advanced we almost always just shot him up more as we approached him. Better safe than sorry.

Then we packed up and moved off a ways so the enemy wouldn't have an exact fix on our location. There's nothing worse than getting shot up at night.

This kind of ambush was called "Ranger style". I suppose that was the way Army Ranger's did it but I don't know for sure. Whatever the case, we had great success with it.

LATE SEPTEMBER '69

Not too long after I returned from my stint as a sniper, our squad was set up around a "hooch" on a routine night ambush. The only notable difference between this location and a hundred others was a large rice straw "hay stack" right in front of the "hooch". Also, about forty yards away was a small pond. It was about forty yards long and about fifteen yards wide. The locals had built this pond by building up a dike all the way around it. The dike was about the same height as the rice paddy dikes in the area, maybe twelve inches or so. I guess they stocked the pond with fish for food and probably also used it to water their water buffalo.

Anyway, at some point this night, three VC/NVA had the bad luck to walk by between our ambush location and the little pond that was several yards in front of the "hooch". We spotted them and immediately blew a hasty ambush on them. We did it in the usual way; somebody "popped" a parachute flare and every man in the squad opened up with his weapon cranked to full-auto.

However, on this occasion, our squad also had the bad luck of managing to miss all three of the enemy soldiers in the initial burst of firing. These three "gooks" then managed to crawl around behind the dike that supported the little pond. Even more unfortunately for us, these three guys decided to "go down shooting". The three of them also had fully automatic rifles and they turned those rifles loose on us. We were standing more or less in the open in front of that little "hooch" and were outlined by the light of the illumination flares that our battalion's mortars or artillery were now putting up overhead. We had nothing to hide behind except that little hay stack. All we could do was lay flat on the ground, return fire, and hope for the best while bullets "cracked" by alarmingly close to our heads.

Fortunately, a Cobra helicopter gunship equipped with night vision capabilities was flying nearby on its own night patrol and we were able to get "patched" in to its radio frequency. We called upon it to help us out of our predicament and within a few minutes it was overhead, sizing up the situation. Unfortunately, the pilots sized the situation up incorrectly and they started firing their automatic twenty millimeter cannon on the wrong side of the pond! They were pouring twenty millimeter high explosive rounds down right in front of our faces about thirty yards away. These rounds had an explosive capability somewhat less than a hand grenade, but were slamming down at about the rate of two hundred per minute! A couple of five second bursts of something like this can do a lot of damage, not to mention scare the hell right out of you.

We began calling frantically on the radio to try and get the Cobra called off. We were finally able to do so, but not before it made a second pass at us. It was coming in low enough that we could see it outlined in the light of the illumination flares swinging over our heads on little parachutes. By this time, some of the guys were so pissed and/or scared of being killed by our own support fire that they started shooting at the helicopter as it made its second pass.

Had the cobra not received the word that it was firing practically on top of U.S. troops it would no doubt have made a third pass, especially since it had been receiving fire. I'm sure that the pilots had spotted our muzzle flashes as well, and would have laid their high explosive rounds down right on top of the squad. No doubt, all of us would have been killed or severely injured.

At any rate, when the cobra got word of its mistake, it made its third pass on the far side of the pond, killing all three of the VC/NVA that were shooting at us.

After the cobra broke off contact, our squad carefully formed a skirmish line under the light of the illumination flares and "swept" out toward the pond and the area that the three VC/NVA had been shooting from. We found the three bodies, collected their weapons, and moved out to set up at a different location for the remainder of the night.

Once again, a narrow escape from death! Just another hard day at the office!

Twenty-six "Gooks"

The largest group of VC/NVA we ever actually saw while I was in Viet Nam was twenty-six by our own head count.

Our platoon was out in the general vicinity of the Plain Of Reeds on a routine night ambush patrol. The seven or so guys in my squad were set up right at the intersection of two medium sized canals along with our platoon leader and his two RTO's (radio men). The other squad was set up several hundred yards farther down the canal behind us along with the rest of the CP group (platoon sergeant and medic).

At some point in the night the guard woke us up and told us that some "gooks" were coming toward us. They were walking along the opposite side of the canal from us and were off to our right a little. They were headed right toward the intersection of the two canals and would be crossing the intersecting canal right in front of us.

We set up a hasty ambush and prepared to "blow them away" as they crossed the canal. We were passing the Starlight 'scope around for one last look when somebody said it looked like there were quite a few of them. Our lieutenant looked through the Starlight "scope again and decided there were indeed quite a few of them. In fact, he decided there were so many of them that we couldn't possibly "blow" a "bush" on them without grievous consequences to ourselves.

As they started to come by in front of us it became apparent that our platoon leader had made a good call. We all laid quietly in the brush along our side of the canal, able to see the NVA unit in the moonlight. They weren't more than ten yards from us.

We began counting them as they crossed the intersecting canal. Everyone was "scared spitless" that one of our own would cough, break wind or even move slightly and disturb the brush around us. The more we counted, the more scared we got. We counted twenty-six of them crossing that canal and held our collective breath the whole time!

Finally the last NVA crossed the canal and headed on toward their sanctuary in Cambodia. As soon as that last guy got across the canal our lieutenant started whispering into the radio, calling in the co-ordinates to request an artillery barrage.

A few minutes later, arty started falling at just about where we thought those "gooks" should be, just a couple of hundred yards away from us. If memory serves me, a night flying helicopter gun ship also worked the area over after the arty quit falling on those unfortunate bastards.

We all watched the show with glee in our hearts, hoping that every one of those "gooks" got killed.

The next morning we "swept" through the area of the previous night's arty barrage. If memory serves me, we were all disappointed because we only found a couple of bodies.

To this day, it is almost incomprehensible to me that a lot more of those enemy soldiers weren't killed. Some might say that they probably carried away some of their wounded or dead. I really don't think they did. I sure as hell wouldn't have stopped to help anybody with all those artillery rounds exploding around me!

ALFA TURNS TRICK
ON ENEMY AMBUSH

Alfa Company, which continually shows the effectiveness which earned them the Sat Cong Streamer Award in August, put it to the enemy again on the night of 13 October as they killed three VC.

Operating southwest of Rach Kien, Alfa Company slipped into their night ambush location. "It was 0130 hours when I checked the area with the starlight scope and saw nothing," PFC William R. ●●●●●, rifleman with Alfa 36, commented. "Not a minute later we could see three VC, and they were so close we didn't need a starlight." Porter of Oneida N.Y. alerted the men in his position to the urgent situation. As the Third Platoon prepared to initiate their ambush, the enemy opened up on the Alfa element. Before the enemy had finished the initial burst, Sp/4 Richard W. ●●●●●, M-60 man, rained fire on the enemy with a rapid burst. When the belt ran out, Irvin, to prevent delay, grabbed a M-16 continuing the barrage. "We were putting out so much lead, that we must have changed the landscape," Irvin reported.

After thoroughly routing the enemy, the Third Herd swept under artillery illumination finding heavy blood trails. It took a second sweep at daybreak to reveal the three enemy bodies produced by Alfa's superior fire power.

***

DON'T INVITE TROUBLE

As your Battalion Surgeon, I feel it very necessary to remind you of the importance of maintaining good health while in the Republic of Vietnam. While here, you are exposed to various diseases, a very dangerous one being malaria. Malaria prevention is one of the most stressed health habits that you will encounter in Vietnam and it is extremely important that each person do as

(Contd Col. 2)

DON'T INVITE TROUBLE
(Contd from Col. 1)

much as possible to prevent malaria. The Chloraquine-Primaquine antimalarial tablet is dispensed every Monday to build your body resistance against this disease, and it is of the utmost necessity that you receive the tablet every Monday. The regularity of consuming the C-P pill is what gives you the best protection against malaria. We here at the 5/60th are fortunate to have little problem with malaria, but let's not invite this very unwanted trouble. Take the C-P pill every Monday and maintain good personal health.

STEPHEN A. ●●●●●
BATTALION SURGEON
***

LOOK OUT! THEY'RE MOVIN' IN

This week the 5/60th received 13 new men. There were three Lieutenants who will become Platoon Leaders, one Staff Sergeant, four Sergeants, and five PFC's. The five PFC's are 91Alfas or as most people know them, Medics. They will be assigned to the various companies where a need exists. With their arrival the Battalion once again approaches full strength in the field of Medical Personnel.

The new men are:

2LT Joseph ●●●●●, Co B, ●●●●●, N.C.
2LT Emerson ●●●●●, Co A, ●●●●●, U.
2LT Morris ●●●●●, Co B, ●●●●●, Ca.
SSG Douglas ●●●●●, Co C, ●●●●●, Mich.
SGT Donnie ●●●●●, Co C, ●●●●●, Va.
SGT Franklin ●●●●●, Co B, ●●●●●, MI
SGT Javier ●●●●●, Co A, ●●●●●, Cal
SGT Francis ●●●●●, Co D, ●●●●●, Ind
PFC George ●●●●●, HHC, ●●●●●, Ark
PFC Charles ●●●●●, HHC, ●●●●●, Ga.
PFC David ●●●●●, HHC, ●●●●●, Fla.
PFC Ronald ●●●●●, HHC, ●●●●●
PFC Michael ●●●●●, HHC, ●●●●●, Pa.
***

Copy of Dad's battalion's weekly newspaper, dated October 17, 1969. We found it at the bottom of his old duffle bag in a pile of papers. The papers included old letters from home, his orders assigning him to his units in Viet Nam and this old battalion newspaper. He obviously kept it because his name was in it.

The "Sat Cong" streamer referred to in the article was awarded each month to the company in the battalion that had killed the most enemy soldiers for the month. "Sat" means killed. "Cong" refers to communist soldiers. Thus, "Sat Cong" roughly means Viet Cong soldiers killed.

OCTOBER, 1969

BATTALION NEWSPAPER ARTICLE

I'm sorry, but I have no memory of this incident. We "blew" so many ambushes. I have no idea how many ambushes we initiated during my year in Viet Nam.

I always thought that my squad "blew" well over two dozen ambushes. I recently spoke to a friend of mine that came "in country" in late January of 1970. We were in the same platoon until I left in very early May. When I told him that I thought the squad had "blown" about two dozen "bush's", he said, "Hell, Rick, we "blew" that many while you and I were over there together". That was about three months!

I think he over-exaggerated it a little bit. However, I have revised my estimate since that conversation. It is now my opinion that my squad probably "blew" about three to three and a half dozen ambushes during my year in Viet Nam.

As for the newspaper article, I can vaguely remember talking to the "PR" guy once about "blowing" an ambush. The article was written in October of '69 and that's when I was carrying the machine gun in my squad. I have no memory of following any "blood trails" ever at night and I have no memory of ever running out of machine gun ammo and having to pick up an M-16 to continue shooting.

Some things I remember very well and other things I just can't recall correctly or at all after forty years. This book should have been written twenty years ago!

Sometimes they shot back when we ambushed them

Sometime in October, I believe, we were out on what we thought would be a routine night ambush patrol. I was carrying the M-60 machine gun at the time. We went about the patrol in the usual way, stopping before dark several hundred yards short of our objective to keep it under observation until after dark and eat a cold c-ration dinner as we waited.

After darkness set in, we moved out to our night location which happened to be an old abandoned one room "house" made of some kind of mortar or something like that as opposed to the usual rice straw "hooch". Probably some well-to-do landowner had once lived in it before the war drove him out. It had a dirt floor and the roof and three sides of it were mostly blown away by shelling in the past. However, it did offer a good view of an area we were interested in, so our squad and half of the CP group set up in it for the night.

The old house sat alongside what might pass for a "road" in Vietnam. It was really just a rice paddy dike that was about six feet or so wide. It had a double set of "ruts" in it where local farmers occasionally pulled two-wheeled carts with water buffaloes. It was so rough that I doubt a jeep could have traversed it.

The area that we were interested in was behind the old house. The rear wall, which was still more or less intact, had two windows in it. From these windows, and by stepping out of either end of the house (the side walls were all but gone), we could observe a rice paddy that was surrounded on three sides by wood lines. The wood line directly behind the rice paddy was about one hundred yards away and was actually part of a rather large patch of jungle. The wood lines on either side of the paddy were thinner, more like thick hedgerows. They both led from the jungle area up toward the "road" we were at. One intersected the "road" about seventy-five yards or so yards to the right of our position and the other intersected the "road" about fifty or so yards to the left of our position. Thusly, this rice paddy was "boxed in" on three sides by woods and our position at the old house was situated at the forth side. Much enemy movement had been reported in this area.

Sometime later in the night the guard awakened us and said there were a "couple of gooks" crossing the rice paddy. We hastily prepared our ambush. I set my machine gun up in one of the open windows. An M-79 man, wanting to share the window with me, set up just to my right. We had already hooked together about one thousand rounds of ammo for the machine gun when we had arrived earlier in the evening, so I was ready. The starlight 'scope was passed to me for a quick look before we "blew" the "bush". It was a common practice to give as many people as possible a quick look, especially the machine gunner, so we had a good idea as to exactly where to trigger our initial burst of fire until a "pop" flare opened to illuminate the area. I took a quick look and noted two VC/NVA about half-way out in the rice paddy, walking from our right to our left.

When I heard the squad leader hit the flare on the ground to fire it and send it skyward, I opened up, trying to shoot quick short bursts out into the paddy at what I thought would be about knee-high at thirty or forty yards.

As soon as the parachute flare opened I could see two enemy soldiers in the rice paddy, running bolt upright in opposite directions. One was going toward the wood line on the left and the other one was heading back toward the wood line on our right. I began tracking the one headed off to the left, zeroing in on him with my tracers. Everyone else was shooting at these guys as well. The first VC/NVA that I was shooting at soon went sprawling into the rice paddy, obviously hit hard. I turned the machine gun to the right and triggered bursts toward the second VC/NVA just as he was about to gain the cover of the wood line.

At about this time I could also see the muzzle-flash of an automatic weapon firing at us from just inside the wood line near where the second "gook" was about to disappear. I headed my tracer rounds toward the area that the muzzle flashes had been coming from and continued to pour fire into the woods.

As it turned out, there were more than two VC/NVA. Bullets were smashing through the "mortar" wall we were behind. Some of the guys in the squad had been standing outside the house at the open ends of it and were shooting when we first "blew" the "bush". Now that we were receiving fire they were scrambling back inside, seeking what little cover the wall could provide.

All of a sudden the situation began to look serious. There were now possibly enemy soldiers on either side of us and we were in danger of being flanked. They could work their way up the wood lines toward either side of our position and be able to fire directly into us as the old house had no walls at either end. Apparently our guard had not noticed the "gooks" when they first came out into the rice paddy. He must have noticed the middle of the column of an undetermined number of VC/NVA who were crossing the rice paddy. We only knew that there were three of them for sure and had no idea how many may have already gotten into the wood line on our left.

The automatic weapon on our right quit firing so I turned the machine gun toward the woods on our left and began to pour fire in that direction. Everyone else in the house was still firing, some towards the left and some towards the right. I continued to fire burst after burst into the wood line as fast I could pull the trigger, letting off for only "milliseconds" between bursts. We were trying to put suppressive fire into both wood lines to discourage any VC/NVA trying to sneak up on us.

I had put several hundred rounds down the barrel by now and the air-cooled machine gun was getting hot. A streak of flame about a foot long was shooting out of the ejection port on the side of the gun. It began to burn the guy on my right that had been sharing the window with me and he had to move to avoid being seriously burned.

Finally, as we were no longer receiving any incoming fire, a cease fire was called. I had, by this time, put about eight hundred rounds of ammo through that machine gun. The weapon was starting to "cook-off" rounds and I had to twist the belt of ammunition to get it to quit firing.

The machine gun had gotten so hot that when it's automatic feeding system chambered a round, the round was literally exploding in the chamber due to the heat and sending the bullet down the barrel. The automatic feeding system then chambered another round and the process would repeat itself. Taking my finger off the trigger could no longer stop the gun from firing. That's why I had to twist the belt of ammo to break the cycle.

The barrel of the machine gun was so hot that it looked rather transparent. Under the light of the illumination flares the barrel appeared to have a white coat of dust on it. The metal must have been turning white-hot. As I moved the gun about we thought we could see the gas plug in the lower barrel assembly moving back and forth inside it's "barrel". Now, metal must really have to be hot to be almost transparent! It's a wonder I didn't ruin that machine gun.

We didn't risk "sweeping" out into that rice paddy. We knew that there was a body out there because we could see it. We also feared that we might get caught in a cross-fire from the wood lines if any VC/NVA were still in them. It was simply too dangerous to be worth the risk and we were now low on ammo anyway after so much shooting.

We packed up and moved away from that old shot-up, half torn down house and relocated our ambush position in a safer place a few hundred yards away.

I don't remember us having any more trouble that night.

*Carrying the M-60 Machine gun. Note the fragmenta-
tion and smoke grenades prevalent on everyone's web
gear. Belts of machine gun ammo around the waist
or over-the-shoulder was a common way to carry the
ammo, although it was sometimes carried in metal
ammo boxes that were secured to the aluminum frame
of a rucksack. Also note soldier with his back to camera.
He is carrying the PRC-25 radio, called a "Prick-25"
by the soldiers that had to lug it around in addition to
all their other gear. Smoke grenades can be seen hanging off of the radio as well as a canteen on the left side.*

Picture of a house similar to the one spoken of in the last chapter. Most Vietnamese were very poor and lived in one-room, dirt-floored thatch huts made of rice straw. The house pictured could only have belonged to a rich person by Vietnamese standards. Note the single "masonry" type wall that is still standing.

Friendly artillery fire - DATE UNKNOWN

L ate one afternoon, after having spent a few days in the "bush" patrolling all day and pulling ambush patrols every night without a break of any sort, we were told that we could take a very rare break from our nightly ambush patrol duty. We were directed to a nearby C.I.D.G. (Civilian Irregular Defense Group) camp so we patrolled our way to the little compound that served to protect the nearby farm village.

The "soldiers" in this compound consisted of those local males either too young to be drafted by the A.R.V.N. Army (seventeen or under) or too old to still be in their Army (forty-five or older). They were mostly armed with old WWII vintage M-1's, good weapons for their time but lacking the ability to fire fully automatic. The C.I.D.G. served two purposes. One, they provided a modicum of protection for the little villages they were built next to and two, it kept track of the local young males to try and prevent them from joining the Viet Cong.

In my opinion these camps didn't accomplish either purpose very well. The camps were too poorly equipped and undermanned to withstand any determined attack and the guys in these camps knew it. They usually either turned their heads the other way or just flatly disappeared when the VC/NVA came around. We also suspicioned that most of them were already recruited by the VC and spent as much time setting booby-traps and sniping at us as they did protecting their local village.

These little compounds were actually made of mud. When the Mekong Delta mud dries it becomes almost as hard as concrete. It took artillery, bombs, or at least a LAW rocket to blow these bunkers up when we encountered enemy soldiers holed up in them.

Anyway, this compound was no more than about fifty yards square. It had a "berm" (wall) of mud built around it that was about six feet high. It was about twelve feet thick at the bottom and tapered off to about four or five feet thick at the top.

In the center of the compound stood a single mud bunker about fifteen yards long and maybe ten yards wide. The inside dimensions were much smaller. Up on the "berm", in each of the four corners, was a small, sand-bagged fighting position. Around the outside of the little "fort" were some strings of barbed wire and coils of concertina wire.

That's all there was to these compounds. There were no troop quarters at all unless the occupants had, of their own accord, erected a couple of very small shelters made of things like empty cardboard c-ration cases and perhaps a poncho for a roof.

Now, what I just described may not sound like much (and it wasn't) but it sure looked good to us. We were not only going to get the night off, we were going to have someone else pull guard duty for us. We could also heat up our c-rations for a change and have hot food if we could find any material to build some fires with. We considered this to be a pretty good deal at the time. Someone broke out a deck of cards and some of the guys played cards for a while until it got too dark to see.

So, as there was no electricity to speak of in Vietnam, and we wouldn't want a light on anyway, considering the fact that the VC/NVA would just use it as a target, we "crashed" shortly after dark.

Sometime during the night, we were jolted awake by a major explosion just outside the berm. It scared us out of our wits, and we all grabbed for our rifles, but stayed flat on the ground. We didn't know what was going on.

As it turned out, one of our own artillery units had fired the round that exploded just outside, and I mean just outside, of the little camp. The round probably had landed no more than fifty yards from us. A one hundred-five millimeter H.E. round has a lot of explosive compound in it and makes for a big explosion when it goes off. It shook the earth beneath us and the sound was deafening. Debris rained down upon us. If it hadn't been for the thick, mud "berm" we would have no doubt suffered some casualties from the concussion and shrapnel that the arty round generated.

What had happened was very simply a mistake. Someone in the arty unit had received a "fire mission" and had just accidentally juxtaposed a couple of the coordinates numbers when relaying the info to the gun crew. When the gun crew fired, the round came down almost on top of us instead of going to where it was intended.

Incidents such as this were referred to as "friendly fire". I'm sure it probably took us a few minutes to get back to sleep afterwards. I bet everybody felt the need to urinate and have a cigarette first also, but I don't remember for sure anymore.

A picture of the "forlorn" little C.I.D.G. camp. At the forefront of the picture is the mud "berm" dad spoke of. The artillery round landed just past the "berm".

"Bushing" the sampans - artillery interruptus

One of the night ambushes that sticks out in my mind is the night we "bushed" a couple of sampans (small boats) near the intersection of a couple of canals. It sticks out in my mind because we were nearly killed by our own artillery that night.

We had set up our ambush right at the edge of some canal out near the Plain Of Reeds. Sometime during the night these two sampans full of supplies and VC/NVA came by, quietly "poling" their way along.

We were right above them on the bank and opened up on them at point-blank range. Our squad leader had signaled us to open up in the usual way, by "popping" a parachute flare. We all laid into those two sampans with everything we had, firing all our weapons on full-automatic, as usual.

As we were pouring fire into these "gooks" the artillery, as usual, shot "lum" for us. Usually the flares went off, up high, a little in front of us and a little to one side.

One little thing went wrong! On this night, for whatever reason, the flares started "popping" directly over our heads. We could still see okay, but, since we were directly under the flares, the "debris" from the exploding artillery shells rained down directly on us.

The explosions themselves were not a problem as they were small ones, just large enough to break open the shell containing the flare and parachute.

The problem was the base plates of the spent rounds that were sent hurtling to earth by the force of the explosions. These things were made of metal, were about the size of a dinner plate, and were about a half an inch thick. I don't know how much they weighed but they would have killed us if they hit us on the head and would have crippled us had they hit us anywhere else on our bodies.

As these base plates came down they made a "whoo-whoo-whoo" sound and then thudded into the earth all around us, some only missing us by a few feet.

There was nothing we could do except cease firing on the sampans and lay flat on the ground, our arms over our heads.

It scared us, and I mean it scared us "spitless". All thought of killing the nearby enemy soldiers disappeared from our minds as we laid motionless on the ground, praying that none of the base plates would hit us. There was nowhere to run to try and get away from them. We were out in the middle of "Indian country" (enemy territory) and to run off into the dark would have been more suicidal than staying "put" and toughing it out, so we just had to lay there and "sweat it out".

Our radio man finally contacted our lieutenant to explain the situation. The lieutenant then finally contacted the arty fire direction center and got the "lum" called off or adjusted, I don't remember which.

That whole process of contacting everybody only took about a minute or so but it was one of the longest minutes of my life! I bet over a dozen of those base plates rained down on us before we could get anything done about it.

I don't remember how the ambush turned out. I think we got one of the sampans and it's occupants and the other one got away.

What I do remember is being scared half to death and extremely pissed-off!

As usual, we packed up afterwards and moved a few hundred yards away to re-deploy our ambush at a new location.

Just another tough day at the office! Just one more near-death experience! The Viet Nam war was really starting to get on my nerves!

December 27, 1969

My platoon moved to a little base camp that may have been named Fire Support Base Gettysburg. It was the 26th day of December, 1969. It was a forlorn little place about one-half mile from the Cambodian border and sat right in the middle of a major enemy infiltration route leading toward Saigon. It sat along a canal in the Plain Of Reeds. The place was about thirty yards wide and about one hundred yards long.

FSB Gettysburg was a new place that had just became operational a few days before we were assigned to it and there was nothing but a small, sand-bagged bunker and three pieces of artillery there when we arrived. Not even a tent! We put the first one up while we were staying there. It was going to be cold c-rations and nightly ambush patrols for the next ten days.

The only upside to the whole deal was that we wouldn't be doing many daylight patrols as our platoon was to provide the only defense the base had. So, if we did any daylight patrolling at all, we would only be going on short, local patrols. Most of our night ambush patrols would be done within a few miles of the place as well.

Now, the deal was, the 1st Air Cavalry Division had been working around this same area for the past week or so prior to our arrival and hadn't scared up any significant contact with the VC/NVA. Apparently the commanding officer of the battalion of Air Cav guy's had told our battalion commander that there were no enemy soldiers in the area or "his boys" would have dealt with them accordingly. Supposedly, my battalion commander made some kind of bet with the Air Cav commander that "our boys" would do better.

So, to make a long story short, the second night out in this new area, the squad I was in, while on a night ambush, had twelve unfortunate VC/NVA walk by us in the middle of the night. We were set up on a little dry spot that had probably been the location of a rice farmers "hooch" a few hundred years before. There weren't many dikes in this particular area of the Plain Of Reeds so the VC/NVA in front of us were walking in the ankle-deep water about thirty yards or so in front of our position. The guard probably heard them splashing in the water.

Everyone was awakened and we quietly formed a firing line just before the VC/NVA passed in front of us. There were about seven of us in the squad and the Lieutenant and his two radio men were with us as well.

At the squad leader's command (he fired a parachute flare), everyone opened up with everything we had. About a minute and a half later it was all over. The VC/NVA had been caught right in the middle of our "kill zone" and didn't even get the chance to shoot back.

We killed four of them and wounded another one badly enough that he couldn't get away. The rest of them scattered into the night and disappeared.

We actually didn't know how well we had done until we "swept" out into the "kill zone" under the light of the flares. As usual, when we saw a body in front of us we just shot it up more as we approached it, just in case. We didn't trust those little bastards any farther than we could "throw them" and never took any chances.

The only reason we took the prisoner is because we realized he wasn't quite dead when we walked up next to him. He was tore up though. I remember that one of his hips appeared to be broken from a bullet. I don't remember what else was wrong with him but he was pretty shot up.

Anyway, after we had called in our successful ambush our battalion commander was so "tickled" he sent an air-cushioned vehicle (hover-craft) out to pick us up the next morning. He wanted us to bring the bodies and the prisoner back to the base camp. We did as ordered and the battalion CO personally flew out in his chopper to take pictures and look things over.

I hope he collected on his bet.

A close-up picture of Dad. This was taken in December of 1969 at a base camp in the Plain Of Reeds, less than two months after his nineteenth birthday.

JANUARY 1970 - PLAIN OF REEDS

One day in January, 1970, our company was on a routine daylight patrol in the Plain Of Reeds. We were doing our usual thing, just out looking for trouble.

I have described the Plain Of Reeds in previous sections. On maps it is described as a wasteland. In reality, it's a large flat plain near the Cambodian border that was rice farmed hundreds of years ago. Apparently the ground was no longer fertile or perhaps drainage problems developed over the years, I don't know. At any rate, during the Viet Nam war, the Plain Of Reeds was a large, uninhabited expanse of rice paddies. The stagnant water stood ankle to knee deep all year around and reeds about crotch to waist high grew in profusion in all the old rice paddies. Enemy troops used this desolate area extensively to move from their Cambodian sanctuaries to the battlefields of the Mekong Delta.

This area was criss-crossed by countless old hand-dug canals. Some of the canals were large enough and deep enough to put a fair-sized boat in. others were small enough that only a small two or three man sized fishing boat could navigate them. These smaller ones were usually about chest to neck deep on the average infantryman and we could just barely ford them.

One of the other platoons was fording one of these smaller canals on this particular day when, off to their left about one hundred fifty or two hundred yards, a VC/NVA with an automatic weapon opened up on them. He basically just emptied the thirty plus rounds of ammunition in the rifle's magazine at the three guys that were actually in the water. There was quite a bit of scraggly brush about six to eight feet high growing along either side of the canal, so I suppose the guys in the water made the best targets.

They suffered one casualty; the young man was killed instantly by a bullet from the snipers weapon.

Those who were on the banks of the canal immediately began pouring a torrent of automatic rifle, machine-gun, and M-79 grenade launcher fire toward the area that the bursts of fire had come from. After "hosing down" the area where the assassin had shot from, several of the guys on that side of the canal "swept" down to the snipers "nest", "recon-ning by fire" as they neared the suspected location.

They never found a trace of him!

As usual, a medivac chopper was called in. Our friends body was taken away. Then the platoon resumed their pa-trol activity.

As the word spread to the rest of the company I finally found out what happened. It made me wonder what the captain would say in the letter that he would write to the young soldier's mother.

After a little while, I emptied my mind, blocking out all feelings and emotions. An infantryman can only afford to think about the immediate moment. He cannot think about the past, as he will only become homesick and lonely. He cannot think about the future, because his chances of living long enough to have a future are very bleak indeed.

To survive at all, an infantryman must concentrate on the moment, watching every step he takes to make sure he doesn't step on a land-mine or a booby-trap. He must be constantly aware of his immediate surroundings, being ever watchful for an enemies ambushes or snipers. He has little or no time for reflection.

All things materialistic or philosophic are completely meaningless to an infantryman. He owns no personal possessions, and he can have no dreams about anything that could someday be.

An infantryman's life can only be described as a life of survival at its most basic level. His attitude can only be described as pragmatism at its most basic level.

An infantryman can only think about staying alive for one more day.

FEBRUARY 1970

The platoon was walking single-file on a rice-paddy dike just after dark. It was during the dry season and the paddies were all dry. We were headed for a typical objective, a couple of farmer's "hooches", to set up a night ambush position. My squad's assignment was to set up at a "hooch" just in front of us. The platoon's other squad was to continue on a few hundred yards farther to set their "bush" up around some other "hooch". I didn't know it yet, but I was going to be wounded in action before the night was over.

I was walking third in line. The radio man was in front of me and in front of him was our squad leader, walking point. The squad leader was about fifteen yards from our objective when several VC/NVA opened up on us with multiple automatic weapons. I mean they went off right in our faces at point-blank range!

At least one automatic weapon was directly in front of us and was being fired right straight down the dike into our column. Bullet's from that weapon were flying right past my head no more than an inch or two away. They were "cracking" by my ear's so close that it sounded like the weapon itself was being fired right next to me.

Another automatic weapon was just off to the right of the first one about ten yards. It was pouring a cross-fire into the front of our column. Tracer rounds from that weapon were passing right in front of my face, just inches from my nose.

The two guys in front of me both went down, badly wounded. Why I wasn't hit in that cross-fire only God Knows. I must have had an Angel on my shoulder!

I had nowhere to go and no other choices now, as I was the closest one to the enemy position and everyone else was directly behind me and momentarily unable to fire without hitting me. I had to react quickly or I was going to die. I didn't even have time to "hit the dirt" . I trained my M-16 on the place where I had seen the muzzle blasts directly to my front and let go on full-auto, with one foot down in the rice paddy and the other foot still up on the dike.

As I was changing the magazine in my rifle, someone came up beside me on my left and threw a concussion grenade toward the VC/NVA to our front. We had to use concussion grenades at such close range to prevent injuring ourselves with the fragments that a "frag" grenade would generate.

I got another magazine in my rifle and began to blast away at the automatic weapon off to our right front as the guy next to me readied another concussion grenade. By the time I had emptied my second magazine, he was throwing the second grenade at the position directly in front of us.

Thankfully, someone behind me was "popping" an illumination flare and we would be able to see better in about two seconds.

Also, the machine gunner and another guy had, by now, been able to get up on line with us to our left. When the flare "popped" open and gave us light, those two guys opened up on the enemy position in front of us while I "hosed down" the weapon on our right front one more time.

Under the light of the flare, we could see several VC/NVA disappearing around the corner of the "hooch". All four of us started pumping rounds right through that little hut, just trying to get lucky.

After that I quit shooting and bent down to look at the wounded radio man who was laying, quite literally, right between my feet.

I could tell immediately that he was hurt badly. He was lying on his right side in the rice paddy, his face pressed up against the dike. I could see the dark stain of blood on his left arm, spreading down his shirt and across his chest. I hated to do it, but I had to roll him onto his back to get to the radio handset. I needed to call back to the CP group, about thirty yards behind us, to get the medic. Our squad leader wasn't moving either, and that was usually a bad sign.

By the time I had put down the radio handset the other guys were "wrapping up" the fire fight. The enemy had disappeared into the rice paddies behind the "hooch" and now was not the time to give chase. Chasing armed men through rice paddies in the dark is just not good soldiering. It was just too dangerous. Artillery was by now providing our illumination and one could never tell when he might get "blacked out" between flares. It rarely happened, but it did happen.

The medic came up right away and we started doing what we could for the wounded while the CP group called in a dust-off to come out in the middle of the night to pick up our wounded. We brought the medivac down in the usual way, holding a strobe-light in an open field, it's search-light outlining us for everyone in miles to see.

I'd like to say that this was the end of an already bad night but it wasn't. We still had an ambush to do. We backed down the dike we had walked up on and set our am-bush location up in the rice paddies about fifty yards short of our original destination. The other squad also found a new place nearby to spend the night.

I was also informed that I was to be the new squad leader as I was the most senior man in the squad now. I had about one month's seniority on the guy that had taken over on the radio and over four month's seniority on the machine gunner. The rest of the squad was all brand new guys.

I knew it was coming, I just didn't really want the job. It involved walking point, something I had already done for over a month in my first unit when I was a new guy. I also didn't want the extra responsibility. I had just turned nineteen about three months prior and I guess the idea of the added responsibilities just kind of overwhelmed me.

Anyway, I picked a guy for first watch and settled down amongst the hard, dried up dirt clods in the rice paddy be-tween my machine gunner and the guy now assigned to the radio. The platoon leader and his two radio men stayed with us since the squad was now down to about five or six guys.

I don't think I had even fallen asleep yet when the new guy I had posted as first guard shook my shoulder. He whispered to me that he thought somebody was coming down the dike from the direction of the "hooch" where we had just gotten shot up at. I grabbed my rifle, sat up, and took a look through the Starlight 'scope. Sure enough, there was a "gook" squatted down on the dike not ten feet away! Behind him several yards was another one.

Apparently the enemy soldiers in the area must have thought that we had all left on the chopper that came in to pick up our wounded personnel. It also was not unusual for VC/NVA to come back around after a fire fight to look for things that G.I.'s had inadvertently dropped or left behind, like a grenade or an over-looked can of c-rations. "Gook re-supply" was what we called it. We tried to be careful about leaving things lying around after a fire fight, but it was hard to get everything accounted for in the dark.

Anyway, this "gook" was now getting so close to me that we could see each other in the darkness, and my guys were still getting their weapons and ammo together and trying to form a hasty firing line. The enemy soldier stepped off the dike he was on and I could see him raising his weapon at me. He was so close I could, honest to God, hear him click the safety switch on his American made carbine to the "fire" position. I couldn't wait any longer. I laid in to him at point-blank range on full-auto and gave him the entire eighteen rounds in several short, two to three round bursts. Then I grabbed a hand-held parachute flare, slammed the bottom of it on the dike to fire it, and hopped over the dike as it "sizzled" skyward, re-loading my rifle as I went.

That flare "popped" open and we could see that VC/NVA running right across our firing line not twenty feet in front of us. He had an obvious limp, but he was still making good time. I had shot that entire magazine of ammo at him and only managed to mangle his leg! However, this guy's luck was about to run out.

Not only was I gunning for him, but my machine gunner, a rifleman and the radio man were also now ready on the firing line. That "gook" didn't make another three steps before he went down into the dirt of the rice paddy face first, bullets tearing into him and kicking dirt up around him as we hammered him.

We didn't have time to have too much fun shooting at him though. We could see that other VC/NVA that was on the dike behind the one we had just killed. He was running for all he was worth to get back up to that "hooch" where we had trouble earlier. Also, in the light of the arty "lum", we could see at least two more enemy up by the "hooch" itself and they were commencing to fire at us with their automatic weapons.

The machine gunner, the radio man, a rifleman, an M-79 man and myself all let loose at those two with everything we had. They ceased fire and disappeared behind the "hooch", apparently heading for a safer environment.

We all got "on line" (formed a skirmish line) and swept up past the dead VC/NVA and toward the "hooch". By coincidence, I was walking on the very same dike that we had been on earlier when we got ambushed. I was about ten feet from the "hooch" when a concussion grenade came sailing over the "hooch" and landed right at my feet. I never even saw it, I just heard it hit the ground in front of me. I tried to dive off the dike to "hit the dirt" in the rice paddy to my left, but I never had a chance. The grenade went off almost immediately.

The sensation I had was one of flying straight up into the air, spinning like a top. I'm sure the spinning sensation was probably just a psychological effect produced by the concussion to my brain. The next thing that I remembered was laying flat on my back, feeling around for my rifle. Someone was standing over me saying something like "are you all right?"

The blast had knocked me about six feet from where I had been standing when it went off. It had also knocked me unconscious, but only for a brief time.

Anyway, I found my rifle and stood up. My right shin-bone felt like someone had hit it with a ball bat just above my boot-top.

One of the guys in the squad took a look at it with me. A small piece of shrapnel, about the size of a BB had hit the right side of my shin-bone, just above my boot-top. It had then scraped along the bone for about three-quarters of an inch, then exited on the left side of my shin-bone. It hurt like hell! However, there was hardly any blood at all. The piece of metal that passed through my leg had been so hot that it had more-or-less cauterized the wound as it went through.

We put a field dressing on it and let it go at that. It damn sure wasn't worth risking another dust-off in the middle of the night. I had been fortunate that the grenade had been of the concussion variety and not the fragmentation type. I would have been torn up "right proper" had it been a "frag" type grenade.

Besides, we were due to be picked up by trucks the following morning and taken back to our base camp. I figured I could limp along okay until the trucks arrived. Professional medical attention could wait a day, I wasn't going to bleed to death.

By this time, I had been in Viet Nam for more than eight months. "The World" as we called home and the United States, was becoming nothing more than a dim and distant memory of an almost forgotten way of life. Being an infantryman at war now seemed to be about all that I could remember ever having been.

The endless cycle's of patrols, night ambushes and helicopter combat assaults were starting to take their toll on me. I was sick and tired of sleeping in the mud, eating cold c-rations, and pulling guard duty damn near every night.

I was becoming so numb to everything that I didn't even bother to entertain thoughts of ever doing or becoming anything else. Getting shot at and killing people was now my way of life.

As I look back on it forty years later, I think that, while in Viet Nam, I lived in hell and rode the "War" horse of the Apocalypse.

A picture of Dad taken shortly after he was "promoted" to Squad Leader. Note soaking wet clothing from mid upper-body on down. The soldiers in the Mekong Delta were almost constantly wet and muddy due to the harsh conditions and hostile terrain. Skin conditions like "trench-foot", "Ring-worm" and "Jock-itch" (jungle-rot) were a constant problem in the vile swamps and low-land jungle of the Mekong Delta.

Dad "walking point" in the muddy, inundated swamps of the Rung Sat. He was attempting to cross a small river when his R.T.O., walking behind him, took this picture. Seconds after the picture was snapped, he stepped into a deep spot and almost drowned. His Platoon Leader jumped in and drug him to shore, thus saving his life. Dad couldn't swim!

MARCH 12, 1970

My platoon was doing "Eagle Flights" on this day. As the four "slicks" carrying the platoon came into the LZ, we started receiving fire to the right of our line of flight. All the door gunners on the right sides of the choppers opened up. A few seconds later we landed about seventy-five or one hundred yards from the wood line.

Everyone jumped out, ran a few yards away from the choppers and flopped down in the tall grass and reeds growing in the marsh-like area in front of the jungle. Everyone was "freaked out" and expecting the worst. However, as the choppers sped away, the firing in the wood line ahead began to die down, then faded out completely.

A couple of determined enemy snipers with automatic weapons had apparently just been feeling "lucky" I guess. They had opened up on the choppers as they were coming in on the LZ and then stayed around just long enough to empty another magazine each at us as we were scurrying to cover after the choppers had flown away.

I don't remember if we had the wood line "prepped" by arty or not before we formed our skirmish line and cautiously advanced up to the edge of the swampy, low-land type jungle so common in the Rung Sat (loosely translated as Forest Of The Assassins) area we were in. The Rung Sat was a long-time hide-out for the VC/NVA and we were always cautious when working in this area.

After getting into the wood line, we formed into a single-file column and began to patrol through the area. I was walking point and being even more cautious than usual. We knew some enemy soldiers were in the area as we had just been taking fire when we landed. My squad was also full of new guys due to recent booby-trap casualties.

I had, at this time, about nine and one-half months "in country" (combat time in Viet Nam). My machine gunner had about six months "in country". I had two or three guys in the squad with about a month of combat time in and two or three more that had been with us for about a week. The platoon's other squad was in about the same shape. If anything serious happened we were going to be in trouble.

The platoon also had a brand new lieutenant. The captain had been staying with the platoon the past couple of weeks to help the new lieutenant "learn the ropes", but he was on his own now. The captain had other matters of importance to attend to.

I'm definitely not saying that the new lieutenant was or would be a bad platoon leader. I'm just saying that the "learning curve" in Viet Nam was a steep one indeed and it takes everybody a while to learn to do the best they can given the almost impossible situation we were in. Our very lives were at stake on an almost daily basis.

Anyway, we patrolled along with no problems for several hundred yards. I came into a small area that was relatively clear of the usual banana plants, nippapalm, bamboo thickets and other scrubby growth that normally impaired our vision and made movement difficult.

Suddenly, that "sixth sense" that a combat vet has "kicked" in. Things just didn't feel right to me. I called for a halt to scrutinize things up ahead a little closer. Something just didn't "smell" right.

I called the new platoon leader on the radio to fill him in on my misgivings and asked him if we could put some "recon fire" up ahead to see if we could flush out anything. He okayed it so I brought my machine gunner and one of the new guys that I had assigned an M-79 to up on line with me and another new guy that was carrying the radio.

I was in a kneeling position, right knee on the ground and my left elbow supported by my left leg. The other three guys were to my right. Just as I put my rifle to my shoulder and began firing, some VC/NVA opened up on us! I had narrowly avoided stumbling into an ambush!

We exchanged fire for only a brief few seconds before something exploded some yards to my front, driving a piece of shrapnel into my right thigh. I don't know if one of the enemy soldiers had a stolen M-79 and had fired a round at us or if, perhaps, one of them had thrown a hand grenade.

Whatever the case, the outcome was that I had been knocked backward onto my butt and was sitting there with a piece of shrapnel about as big around as the lead of a pencil and about two inches long sticking out of my right thigh. I had just received my second wound in less than six weeks!

I scrambled around behind the nearest tree to get out of the direct line of fire and look myself over. The VC/NVA broke contact pretty quickly but my guys put quite a few more rounds into the jungle ahead just to make sure that the "gooks" got a proper "escort" out of the immediate area.

A medic came up to look me over and advised against pulling the piece of shrapnel out by myself. It was sticking out of my leg about a half an inch, however, and I just couldn't resist pulling it out myself. I figured it would make a great little war souvenir.

A medivac was called and I walked myself out to a nearby open area and crawled aboard when it arrived.

I ended up getting about three or four days off over that little piece of shrapnel. I spent it wisely, loafing about the base camp, sleeping late and smoking pot. I knew I would be back in the "field" soon enough.

Date unknown -1970

I don't remember this incident very well at all. However, the lieutenant that had just taken over our platoon at the time remembers the incident very well and refreshed my memory at a reunion. I will relate the story as best as I can remember and add the platoon leaders comments. I think it is a story worth re-telling.

Our platoon was on a routine night ambush patrol and was "holed up", waiting for it to get dark so we could move into our assigned location.

What makes this night so different is that we had someone along to observe the infantry at work.

It seems that the Air Force, as part of their "jet jockeys" advanced training, made their pilots go along on at least one operation with the lowly "grunts" down on the ground. On this night we had an Air Force captain along with us to observe. Apparently he was just there to see what war was like for us guys down on the ground.

Anyway, just after dark the whole platoon moved out, heading for our two assigned night locations. We hadn't gone far at all when we spotted eight VC/NVA coming out of the jungle about four hundred yards away. They hadn't noticed us and were headed right toward us.

Our platoon leader had us set up a platoon sized "L-shaped" ambush. We had plenty of time to get ready. Two machine guns, three or four M-79's and over a dozen M-16's waited patiently behind a rice paddy dike for those poor unfortunates to get into the "kill zone". The lieutenant was ready on the radio to call arty for illumination at just the precise moment.

The VC/NVA were about ten yards from us when we opened up on them.

It was a turkey shoot! The whole platoon opened up on those "gooks" at once when they walked into the "kill zone". Every weapon in the platoon raked the "kill zone" with fire as the "lum" rounds "popped" open overhead.

After a cease fire was called, we "swept" out into the area in front of us and found three dead bodies and a couple of very heavy blood trails. We really tore those guys up.

As the lieutenant tells the story, this Air Force captain was really impressed.

He commented to our platoon leader that, having always been high above the ground war, he had no idea how "up close and personal" things were down in the rice paddies! He also said that the fire power an infantry platoon puts out was very impressive and that it really scared him to actually be in on what he considered to be the "real deal".

When the Air Force captain left us the next day he told our lieutenant that anytime we ever needed help to just let him know and he would get his people to us ASAP.

I guess we did made an impression on the guy.

For us it was nothing more than another day at the office. Like I said earlier, I didn't really even remember this night until the lieutenant reminded me of it when he told us the story at the reunion.

We "blew" so many "bushes" while I was in Viet Nam that there's no possible way I could remember all of them. Something significant had to have happened on a particular night for me to remember a specific ambush. Had the lieutenant not mentioned the Air Force guy being with us, I wouldn't have recalled it at all.

APRIL 24, 1970

On the morning of April twenty-forth I had just returned from a night ambush patrol. I was on my way over to the chow hall to see if it was still serving food when my first sergeant hollered at me as I passed his little bunker that passed as an office.

I went in to see what he wanted and, to my surprise, he told me that I was finally being relieved of combat duty. You cannot imagine my relief.

I had been almost constantly pulling combat duty for exactly eleven months. I had been wounded twice and, lately, had become as nervous as a cat.

I was suffering from a severe case of combat fatigue (now known as Post Traumatic Stress Syndrome) and just didn't know it. I had been having nightmares lately and was also starting to talk in my sleep, neither of which was good, especially out on night ambush patrols.

I had been having what doctors call "intrusive thoughts". Ever since I had been wounded the second time, the thought that "the third time's a charm" had been running through my mind over and over. I felt that if I got hit again I would almost certainly be killed.

I had also recently developed an almost superstitious aversion to carrying hand grenades. After carrying them on my web gear for the past eleven months with no problems whatsoever, I had suddenly become afraid that the pin on one of them would accidentally become dislodged and the grenade would blow up. This was strictly bizarre thinking on my part. I attached the grenades to my gear by their "spoons" (handles) and, in the highly unlikely event that a pin would work it's way out, the grenade would at least fall off my web gear because the "spoon" separated from the grenade itself when the pin was pulled.

Anyway, the "first shirt" told me to report to the base security sergeant. I was going to stay on the base camp and loaf all day, just monitoring the trickle of civilian foot traffic that came in and out of the gates of the fire base.

When I got to the security bunker, I was given a helmet liner that had been painted a shinny black and had the letters SG (security guard) stenciled on it in white. I was then told to get my rifle and go down to the rear gate of the little fire base and monitor the civilian traffic coming in and going out.

I spent my first day on guard duty watching the trickle of civilians coming and going. I had no idea what to do, but they all knew the drill. When one of them came in they always showed me their I.D.'s. Usually the papers were written in Vietnamese and I couldn't even speak the language let alone read it.

So, having no other instructions, I just let them all in. At the end of the day, I just let them all back out.

On my second day (April twenty fifth) out of the field I did the same thing. The only difference was that I was assigned to the more prestigious front gate. No doubt it was due to my superior performance at the back gate the day before.

On my third day (April twenty-sixth) I was told by the head of security to report back to my company.

The battalion was moving out to a new base camp and all casual personnel (people like me who were performing temporary and/or non-essential duties) were to immediately return to their old companies.

I grabbed my duffle bag, hopped on the next truck headed out, and left the only home I had known for the last ten months.

About an hour later I arrived at the new fire base and reported in to the "first shirt".

The crotchety old "first shirt" told me to stow my duffle bag and get out to the chopper "pad" to await the re-supply chopper that would soon be going out to re-supply the company. They had already been choppered up North about twenty-five miles and were on a patrol somewhere up there.

I was being sent back to the "bush". Twenty-seven days and a "wake-up" left in Viet Nam and I had to return to combat duty. My heart sank!

April 26, 1970

The re-supply chopper I was riding on set down somewhere in the vicinity of the Hobo or Bo Loi Woods. My old company had been patrolling around the area all day and were preparing to go into a night defensive position (NDP) as soon as they got re-supplied.

The guy's were on a company sized operation, something most of them had never done. Our battalion had adopted "Ranger-style" tactics months ago. Most of the guys in the company had plenty of experience in small unit operations of squad and platoon sized groups but little experience in company sized operations that set up for the night in the jungle.

As it turned out, I was now one of the few guys in the company that had any experience in setting up company sized NDP's in the jungle. It was a lot different than setting up a night ambush position.

For one thing, as noted earlier in this text, Starlight 'scopes were virtually useless in the jungle. There just wasn't usually enough ambient light to allow their sensors enough light to amplify. Therefore, we didn't do any night ambushes, which was just fine with me. We simply "circled our wagons" every night and set up a few outposts a couple of hundred yards in front of our location.

I helped show the guys in my platoon how we pulled guard duty months ago down in the Mobile Riverene Force. They learned to sit in the dark with the radio hand-set in one hand and the "clacker" for the claymore mine in the other hand. Rifles were laid across our legs as we sat cross-legged, peering out into the blackness and listening for movement.

Claymore mines were also utilized extensively as a defensive weapon in an NDP. Before we had only used Claymores sporadically at best. Claymores were a shaped charge which was designed to blow in a specific direction as opposed to just blowing in all directions like a hand grenade. However, they still had a dangerous "back blast" so it was necessary to protect yourself from that "back blast".

When we were working in the open rice paddies doing night ambushes, we usually had no way of protecting ourselves from that "back blast" so we often didn't put them out.

Now, since we were setting up in the jungle at night, I knew that we could set the Claymores up just in front of a tree to protect ourselves.

I also knew that the VC/NVA were not above booby-trapping our claymores in the middle of the night. I had long ago been taught to wrap the detonating wire a couple of wraps around the Claymore itself when setting it out in the evening. That way, in the morning, you could just yank on the wire to dislodge the Claymore from the ground.

This avoided getting someone blown up in the morning when they went out to retrieve the Claymore in the remote event that it had been booby-trapped.

Other than that, our new Area of Operations proved unremarkable except that we were now on dry ground all the time and didn't have to go to sleep soaking wet every night. In a matter of days most of our skin problems like "trench foot" began to clear up.

The new AO also was actually more like a forest than a jungle. It consisted basically of single and double canopy tree cover. The ground was relatively clear of the stunted banana plants, bamboo thickets and nippapalm growth that had obscured our vision and slowed our progress down in the delta. We could now move around a little easier and could see ahead of us quite a bit better.

For the next six days I patrolled with my old company, cursing my bad luck and paranoid as hell that I was going to get killed.

Thank God our contacts with the enemy were limited in nature for those six days.

On the seventh day (May 2nd), I received my orders to go home! I was scheduled to leave on May 6th.

I wasn't due to leave Viet Nam until May 24, but I had gotten an eighteen day "drop" from my one year tour of duty. This had become a somewhat common occurrence in Viet Nam by 1970 due to the troop withdrawals as America was turning the war over to the Vietnamese and pulling out. I knew some of the guys had been getting such "drops" off the end of their tours of duty, I just hadn't known it had been happening lately. I just never, in my wildest dreams, thought I could be so lucky. It took me completely by surprise.

When the battalion had moved to it's new location we had been attached to the 1st Air Cavalry Division to assist in the invasion of Cambodia.

That invasion had started on May 1st. Our unit was basically right in the middle of it and things looked like they were just going to get worse.

I had to leave on the re-supply chopper that night. I didn't even have time to say good-bye to the guys I had been serving in Hell with.

On may 8th, six days after I received my orders, I was standing on the front porch of my parents house, home at last. The war was over for me.

It was thirty years later before I even got the nerve up to contact any of those I served with. I just wanted to forget about that damned war.

PART THREE
Odds and ends

A FEW WORDS ABOUT
BOOBY-TRAPS.

I can't tell you how many guys in my platoon alone were lost to booby-traps. The number would have to be somewhere around a dozen and a half, maybe even two dozen. Booby-traps were everywhere.

They usually consisted of something as simple as a grenade (with its fuse shortened to detonate instantly) rigged up with a trip-wire. But, there were all kinds.

I saw one hundred-five millimeter artillery rounds rigged to blow up.

I saw the infamous punji pits. They were just simple holes dug a foot or two down into the ground with dozens of sticks, sharpened at both ends, stuck into the bottom of the hole.

I saw home-made devices made of nothing more than old coke cans or empty c-ration cans and filled with explosive material taken from "dud" bombs or arty rounds, topped off with a fuse.

They usually just used a trip-wire (actually it was usually just a dirty piece of string; cheap and excellently camouflaged by its own dirt) to set them off with but sometimes they rigged up an electric detonator to be able to detonate the device on command. Tripwires were easiest for them and safer too. It was like a little ambush except they didn't have to be anywhere nearby, so there was practically zero risk involved in it for them. There was no maintenance involved either.

They put them across trails, they put them on rice paddy dikes, and they put them just inside the wood lines. They put them everywhere! Let me give you a few examples:

One night we came out of the wood line, as usual, just after dark, and headed out into the rice paddies to set up our nightly ambush position. I don't know how far we had walked, maybe a half-mile or so. Our objective, as usual, was a couple of rice-straw huts in a likely-looking location. A piece of what appeared to be a broken chunk of field tile was lying un-noticed in the dark along the edge of the dike we were walking on. The first two or three guys missed it but then this guy "stubbed" into it. The resulting explosion injured him badly. We heard later that he lost his leg. Unfortunately, the guy walking in front of him took a piece of shrapnel in one of his kidneys.

As usual, we called in the medivacs, fired up the strobe lights, and dusted them off. Then we proceeded on to our ambush site.

On another occasion, we were doing a daylight patrol. I was a squad leader on this occasion, and was walking point with my squad right behind me, followed by the rest of the platoon. We were in the general vicinity of the Plain Of Reeds and had been walking in calf-deep water out in open fields all morning. I came to a little canal or ditch that was small enough to jump over. However, I had been in Vietnam far to long to be so careless as to just "hop" over with out looking first.

I briefly checked out the bank on my side, stepped down into the water, and briefly examined the opposite bank before climbing back up again. I had taught my people to do as I did and walk where I walked, and I expected them to do so.

Anyway, some relatively new guy, who knew better, decided to jump across the canal. He told me at a reunion thirty years later that the doctors said he lost about two and one-half pounds of meat off his legs.

Or, how about the time my platoon was patrolling along a trail in the jungle. My squad was not on point, so about a dozen guys were walking ahead of me. For some reason or another, a brief halt was called. I stopped and happened to look down at my feet. There, under my right boot was a broken, curled up trip-wire. About a foot from my boot was a grenade, tied to a tree. It had the other end of the trip-wire hanging from its ring. Who knows why that wire broke instead of pulling the pin on that grenade. And, who knows which one of us broke the wire.

I got more if you ever want to hear them.

Dad holding a sign pulled from the ground next to a trail that was booby-trapped. The VC in the area were brazen enough to plant a warning sign in English. The hand-painted sign says STOP. A Vietnamese "Tiger Scout" helped him check it out to make sure it didn't blow up when he pulled it out of the ground. The sign had a hand grenade under it's stake, rigged to blow up if some G.I. was dumb enough to pull it up before checking it. Dad was smart enough to check it out before he pulled it up.

MORTARS AND ROCKETS

Mortars and rockets weren't a big deal for me. The guys who stayed in the little base camps and LZ's we built had to cope with that kind of stuff once in a while. The clerks, the cooks, the mortar guys in the company's weapons platoons and the arty guys lived in those places. The base camps were more worth-while targets than a scraggly, under-strength infantry platoon out in the "bush". They were also stationary targets while the infantry was always on the move.

I was only in one rocket attack. When I was first assigned to the 9th Division I spent three or four days at the big division base camp at Dong Tam acclimating to the heat, zeroing in our weapons, and getting a little last minute training. While I was there a couple of rockets came in one night. One of them hit a wooden barracks about two or three doors down from the barracks I was staying in. I don't remember how bad the damage was, but I do know that the barracks was full of new guys going through training with me. A lot of them got hurt badly and their tour of duty in Viet Nam was over before it really began.

The "old" guys around the base camp told us that the enemy was probably trying to hit the fuel supplies at the chopper pad about a quarter of a mile away. At the time I thought that apparently those one hundred twenty-two millimeter rockets either weren't real accurate or else "Charlie" wasn't very good at aiming them.

A few weeks later, when I was in the field, we found one of their rocket launchers. It was nothing more than a wooden "trough" looking affair that was pointed in the direction they wanted to shoot the rocket toward. Elevation was accomplished by propping different sized sticks under the front of it.

I only got mortared when I was staying overnight at a base camp or LZ. I worked out of this one base camp off and on for over ten months. Most of the time we worked a four day cycle that allowed us two nights on the base camp every four days. I remember getting mortared three or four different times. On a few other occasions, I heard guys talking about the mortar rounds that hit "last night". I must have slept right through a couple of other mortar attacks.

These little base camps weren't very big. They were usually circular in design and maybe one hundred fifty yards across. The VC/NVA normally hit us with about four to six rounds and that would be about it. Usually the mortars were of the smaller sixty millimeter variety.

In fact, they sometimes missed the entire base camp with some of their rounds. Of course, if the round exploded ten yards outside the barbed wire and your bunker was situated five yards inside the barbed wire it probably wasn't quite as funny.

At some point in time, some platoon from our company ran across a mortar "emplacement" not far from our base camp. It was nothing more than a little trench dug in the ground. It was about six inches wide, a foot long, and about a foot deep. The end of it that was pointed toward the base camp was slanted at about a twenty or thirty degree angle. This was how the VC/NVA zeroed in on our camp. They simply dropped the mortar tube into the little trench, the angled side designed to give the mortar the exact range and direction. They would then fire off a few rounds, pick up the mortar tube and disappear before any counter-battery fire could be placed on them. Pretty slick, huh!

Dad walking point in the dense low-land jungle common to the Mekong Delta area of South Viet Nam. Note the nearly impenetrable foliage that prevented the troops in the delta from seeing more than a few feet in front of them. The combat "fire-fights" were often very up close and personal in this type of jungle. Enemy soldiers could easily hide and wait until the point man practically stepped on them before "springing" their ambushes. Also note that he is wading in hip-deep water. This picture was probably taken in March of 1970. Note the dark circles under his nineteen year old eyes. The ten plus months of long patrols, night ambushes and "Eagle-Flights" clearly were taking a toll on him.

EQUIPMENT

In the unit I was in, guys wore their equipment pretty much however they wished. Some used rucksacks (usually complete with aluminum frame), some used "butt-packs," like the ones you see the guys using in the movie "Full Metal Jacket", and some did otherwise. I knew a guy in my platoon that used an old gas mask "pouch" to carry his c-rats in. He simply secured it around his waist.

Hardly anyone used those little magazine "pouches" that attached to the front of the web belt. They only held three magazines (four if you laid one on top of the other three and forced the flap to hook shut). The magazines also had a tendency to fall out if you moved around any while under fire and forgot to hook the top down every time you got a fresh magazine.

Web belts and load-bearing suspenders (together they were called a harness) were almost universally worn and practically everybody that carried the M-16 rifle used ammo bandoleers tied around their waist's to carry magazines in.

Helmets were nice to have as they gave you a sense of security when being shot at. After a while though, most of us abandoned our helmets. Being able to move fast in an emergency was of critical importance and helmets tended to fall off constantly when running, crawling through enemy fire, dragging wounded people to safety, etc. Even if you used the chin strap to secure them, they tended to "jostle" around on your head a lot, usually falling down in front of your eyes at a critical moment. So, we tended to ditch them a lot in favor of the ubiquitous "boonie hat". You know, the thing that looks like a fisher-mans hat. It has a little brim all the way around it and is made of a soft, floppy material. It also doubled as a pillow. Granted, a poor substitute for a pillow, but it's all we had.

My personal set-up evolved as I went along, but I eventually sort of settled on the following;

I had a harness consisting of a web belt and a pair of load-bearing suspenders. I was only issued one canteen holder when I first came in country as that was all they could find. I carried a canteen in it on my right hip. On my left hip, I hung a second canteen from the back of the left suspender by using a "D" ring. I put the "D" ring through the little piece of plastic that held the cap onto the canteen.

At the back of my belt, I simply tied a poncho on by rolling it up tightly and securing it to the belt with an extra shoestring. That was my bedroll.

The suspenders had some little metal "rings" on them. There was one on each side up about top-of- your-pocket high and another one on each side down by where they hooked onto the web belt in front. I stuck the "handles" of grenades in them to have plenty of grenades within easy reach. I simply bent the "handles" upward after sticking them through the "rings" and they stayed very secure that way.

Then I took two seven-pocket ammo bandoleers and tied them around my waist, somewhat loosely, so I could get the rifle magazines out easily. I have seen guys tie them too tightly and then not be able to extract the magazines when needed. All we had to do to make them fit right was cut the carrying strap of the bandoleer and then tie the ends of it in a bow behind our backs. We tied them in a bow instead of a knot so we could get them off in an emergency (drowning) and so we could take them off at night.

Counting the magazine in the rifle that gave me fifteen mag's of ammo and up to four grenades on hand. The basic load was supposed to be seven magazines of rifle ammo and two "frags", but, if you have been reading this series of stories, you would know by now why we carried at least double the basic load of ammunition.

Everything was about balancing the infantryman's weight load as best as possible. It was a balancing act between mobility and fighting ability. It was critical to both be able to move fast yet have enough to protect and sustain one's self.

Next would be c-rations.

Both of the units I was in during my tour of duty in Viet Nam were highly airmobile and the infantry guys were definitely perceived as "light" infantry, particularly in view of the horrible terrain we had to cover. Re-supply ships were available almost every night under normal circumstances.

While in the Mobile Riverene Force we started our three day patrol cycle with four c-ration meals. Lunch and dinner on day one and breakfast and lunch on day two. Near the end of day two we received a supply drop of three more rations. We ate dinner that night and breakfast on the morning of day three, leaving us only one ration to "hump" with us until lunch. If we stayed out longer than three days, we usually got a re-supply drop every night.

I had a sock tied to the left side of my web belt. I put the lighter weight c-rats like the cans of crackers in it and let it dangle at my left side.

The smaller, heavier cans of things like shredded turkey or dehydrated ham and powdered eggs I simply put in the bottom two cargo pockets of my shirt.

I carried larger heavy cans (about the size of a soup can) that contained things like peaches or meatballs and beans in an old Claymore bag. I cut the carrying strap of the bag in two and tied the ends of it to the two little canvas "epaulet" thingies that were at the top of the shoulders of my suspenders.

When I moved to 3rd Brigade, which is where I spent most of my year in Viet Nam, our lives revolved around a four day cycle that usually involved night ambushes for the first two nights.

If no real daylight patrolling was involved, we managed to get hot chow from the mess hall pretty regularly before we left for our night ambush patrols and again when we returned the next day. Therefore, we could travel pretty light. In the event we were going to stay out for the two days and do daylight patrols as well as our night ambush patrols, we just took along enough c-rations to last us until the re-supply "bird" arrived the second afternoon.

When we went on an extended seven to ten day stay on the little temporary fire bases, we just had to eat c-rats day after day unless or until some kind of part-time mess tent was set up. Sometimes a mess tent would eventually appear, sometimes it wouldn't. It all depended on how long the patrol base was expected to be operational. However, we were usually re-supplied everyday on these little temporary bases, so we didn't have to "hump" many c-rations if we did end up on an extended patrol.

The real problem was how to heat up our c-rats. We sometimes used the explosive C-Four. It needed both heat and pressure to make it blow up. However, when lit with a match, it burned very hot. A few little pieces about the size of a marble would quickly heat a can of c-rats a little. The Army finally stopped this practice as we were using up too much of their explosives. They never provided us with any other means of heating the food though, so we ended up eating our c-rations cold most of the time.

Anyway, after throwing my load bearing web gear on and tying my bandoleers of ammo around my waist I had my "basic" load together.

All I needed to do then was put my "extra" gear on!

Even as a squad leader, I almost always carried a hundred round belt of machine gun ammo over one shoulder and the Starlight 'scope over the other shoulder. I also always carried two or three parachute flares in the lower left cargo pocket of my pants. They were essential for "blowing" "bushes".

The other guys in the squad also had to divide up our equipment as well as carry their own "basic" loads.

Someone had to carry the PRC-25 radio. Someone had to carry the machine gun. Someone had to carry the Claymore mine and the required one hundred foot rope assigned to each squad.

Each squad also had to carry a minimum of one thousand rounds of ammo for the machine gun. Usually two guys in the squad were designated ammo bearers for the machine gun and therefore had to carry between three hundred and four hundred rounds apiece. That was what new guys usually got assigned to because four hundred rounds of machine gun ammo weighed in at about twenty-four pounds! It was a heavy load in addition to their "basic" loads but it also kept them in the middle of the squad column which was a safer place to be when you knew next to nothing about staying alive in a combat zone.

I always thought it was bull-shit that I had to walk point when I was a new guy. I had no idea what was going on and only survived that first month by the greatest of luck and the Grace of God. I did become a better soldier because of it though.

Anyway, the forty to sixty pound loads we carried on our backs all day made life difficult.

Add in "humping" through knee-deep mud all day in ninety-five degree heat and ninety plus percent humidity (feels like temps of one hundred ten degrees) and you have a perfect recipe for exhaustion and heat prostration.

Yeah! Light infantry!

A good picture of dad "taking a break". Some of the equip-ment carried by the individual soldier is revealed in this photo. Extremely worn combat boots in lower left are sitting just in front of the parachute flares used to initiate am-bushes. His canteens (the guys usually carried two or three) are visible and on the ground in front of him are stacks of rifle magazines for his M-16. The camouflaged item under his feet is a poncho liner. It was an extremely light blanket that most of the guys carried during the dry season to cover up with at night to help keep the mosquitoes off them. It was too hot in the Mekong Delta to use a cover at night for any-thing except keeping the bugs away from exposed areas like the face and hands. He is cleaning his Starlight 'scope with one of his socks. The grey item in the center of the picture is an inflatable rubber mattress (they called it a "rubber bitch"). They weren't used to sleep on at night because they squeaked when laid on. Each squad carried one or two for

use in crossing the deep canals and rivers that laced the Mekong Delta. Guys like him that couldn't swim would "straddle" the mattress and cross the river by holding on to a rope. He said that the guys who crossed that way usually had two or three rifles slung over their necks as well as other equipment piled up in front of them on the mattress. This equipment belonged to the guys that could swim. He would have drowned instantly had he ever fallen off the mattress in one of those many river crossings, due to multitude of rifles and equipment he was weighted down with.

On patrol, probably in Long An Province. Note the Claymore mine bag slung over one shoulder and the wound bandage being used as a strap to carry the Starlight 'scope. Also note the little one log "bridge" the locals used to ford the muddy spot. This picture was probably taken in the early AM, as shirt is buttoned up at neck and sleeves are not rolled up. It was a common practice to button up tightly at night to aid in protecting against the hordes of malaria-bearing mosquitoes.

UNIFORMS

All the infantry guys I ever saw wore the standard "tropical issue" combat uniform.

The pants had the two "bellows" type cargo pockets on the sides of the legs and the other four pockets normally associated with men's pants. The rear pockets had a button and flap on them if memory serves me and the cargo pockets had two buttons and a flap on each one. The pants also had little draw strings at the bottom of the legs so you could pull them tight to help keep out mud, mosquitoes and leeches. The draw strings never did a very good job at any of the three things they were designed to do.

The shirts had four pockets, each held closed by a flap and two buttons. The top two pockets were slanted downward toward the middle of your chest. The bottom pockets were aligned so as to be straight across if memory serves me. All four of the shirt pockets were of the "bellows" type.

We didn't have camouflage clothing or "tiger stripe" clothing. Only the "glory units" like Navy S.E.A.L.'s or "recon" guys wore that stuff. In the jungles of Viet Nam, you couldn't see a guy in an orange "jump suit" fifteen yards away.

When I was in the Mobile Riverene Force we got a change of clothes about every other time we came in from a three day operation. The Navy guys usually just sat a box full of shirts, a box full of pants, and a box fill of socks out in our troop compartment.

The stuff was all used clothing. Mostly it was stuff that guys in the rear area no longer wanted. I'm not saying that the infantry guys were intentionally treated as "second class citizens", it's just that the guys in the rear were held to a higher standard of dress than we were and were expected to look half-way decent. Out in the infantry, the same clothes were worn for long periods of time and were subjected to a hard life anyway. Why give us the "good" stuff.

The shirts rarely had any kind of insignia on the sleeves. Most of that kind of stuff was never put on these clothes or had been taken off before being issued to us. Sometimes a button or two was missing and an occasional small hole might be found in some of the stuff, but it was generally serviceable.

The clothing deal was a little different after I got re-assigned to a real base camp. Since I only had the clothes on my back when I got to my new home, the supply sergeant had to issue me some extra clothing. He gave me three or four sets of fatigues that were of about the same quality as the stuff I had been wearing down in the MRF.

The big difference was that I was now responsible for getting my own clothes cleaned. Fortunately, some enterprising locals had set up a little laundry shop at our base camp.

I could take my clothes down to it and they would send them out to some other local civilians to have them cleaned. Apparently they washed the clothes in a local river or canal because they still stunk to high heaven when we got them back. However, the mud was washed off them so it was better than nothing. They would also sew on your rank and other insignia, for a price, if you wanted them to. I rarely bothered with that since no one seemed to care if us infantry guys were "strack" or not.

Socks had to be begged from the supply sergeant. He always acted like he was giving us his last pair and we often had to complain to the first sergeant to get socks. Since the first sergeant didn't seem to like me, I had to sometimes resort to bribery to get socks.

The supply sergeant was a serious alcoholic and in Viet Nam all the G.I.'s were issued ration cards that only allowed the purchase of a few bottles of hard liquor per month. Since I was never in a base camp that was large enough to have a PX that stocked hard liquor, my ration card went unused.

The supply sergeant, however, often got out of our little base camp and went to larger bases to obtain supplies. Therefore, he could get hard liquor. His problem was the limited amount that his ration card would allow. My problem was getting socks. Therefore, I cut a deal with him. He could use my ration card all he wanted if I could get all the socks I wanted. Problem solved. He stayed drunk and I had socks.

As for boots, I wore the same pair for the entire year I was in the "bush" in Viet Nam. They got wet and muddy on a daily basis. I "humped" countless miles on them and slept with them on my feet most nights. The soles were badly worn and the uppers had holes in them, but they made it all the way. The Army buys good boots.

Never once did they get polished until the day I left Viet Nam to come home. They wouldn't let me on the airplane unless I got them polished. All of a sudden the Army cared about me again. How thoughtful!

I still have that pair of boots and treat them with "war souvenir" status.

SNAKES

I hate snakes. They scare me. I've always been afraid of them.

When I first arrived in Viet Nam someone told me that of the one hundred twenty-seven types of snakes known on earth, one hundred twenty-six of them were represented in Viet Nam. He said that the only type of snake not found in Viet Nam was the rattlesnake family. I don't know if the guy was right or not, but I do know that Viet Nam's jungles were full of snakes.

I personally saw two Cobra's (one in captivity), countless light green Bamboo vipers, and often saw a species that looked a lot like a Water Moccasin. Another type of snake that I frequently saw was a non-poisonous constrictor of some kind. I think it was called a Mangrove Snake. It had two colors around it. One of the colors was yellow and, if I remember correctly, the other color was either brown or black. I also don't remember if it's colors were banded or spotted.

Among the poisonous snakes that I infrequently saw was one that we called a Krait snake. I don't know if that was it's correct name or not. It had black and white bands on it and was considered very dangerous. We generically referred to this snake as a "two-stepper". Supposedly, after being bitten by this snake, a man could only take two steps before going down. This was probably just G.I. folklore, but we didn't take any chances.

Another type of snake, infrequently seen yet none-the-less present, was one called the Russell's Viper. It was a light brown snake with dark ring-like designs on it. We were told that this snake was as dangerous as a Cobra. It seemed to like to sneak around in the rice paddies more so than in the jungle.

I could set and tell snake stories all night long.

Once, at a night ambush site during the rainy monsoon season, our squad was set up for the night on a large grave. We were there because the "well-to-do" Vietnamese put their dead in above water graves due to the high water tables in the area. It was raining and the paddies were brim-full of water.

I was sitting at the top of the grave mound pulling my stint on guard duty. The other five or six guys were laying on the sides of the grave in a circle around me. I began to hear the "rustling" sound of someone wiggling around in the plastic poncho that each of us carried to roll up in at night to try and keep some of the rain off of us. A few moments later a guy stood up, unwrapped himself from his poncho, and started shaking his left pant leg. Out slithered a snake about two feet long.

" God-damned snake" said the G.I. Then he wrapped his poncho back around him and laid back down!

No way could I have been that calm about that!

I worried about that snake for the rest of my guard shift. I continued to worry about it afterwards as I lay on the grave wrapped up in my poncho. Only exhaustion allowed me to get any sleep at all that night.

On another occasion, when we were just settling down into our night ambush location, I felt something in the small of my back when I first laid down. Thinking it was a stick or something, I reached behind my back to feel for and remove the foreign object. At first I thought I felt something, then decided I didn't. When I pulled my arm out from under me, a big snake over two feet long was wrapped around my left fore arm .It was too dark to tell what kind of snake it was, but I thought it looked a lot like the American Water Moccasin.

Now, noise discipline was imperative on a night ambush and movement needed to be kept to a minimum as well, mind you.

I'm sure you can imagine what started expletives started coming out of my mouth. I immediately jumped up and began shaking my arm to rid myself of the loathsome and unwanted visitor.

Due to a bright moon, I saw the snake hit the ground and crawl under the guy laying next to me. When I informed him of the situation at hand, he immediately jumped up, threw his poncho aside and together, we started hammering at the snake with the butts of our rifles. The trouble was, he was too fast for us. It slithered away from us and crawled under yet another guy.

We informed this third fellow of the predicament that he was now in, so he threw back his poncho, jumped up, and joined us in the pursuit of the elusive little devil, adding the butt of his rifle to the fray. Now, three of us were cursing and pounding the ground with our rifle butts, creating enough noise and confusion to make everybody in the squad start cussing. I'm sure if any enemy soldiers had been nearby, they could not have missed the fact that we had an ambush set up in the area.

To shorten an already long story, the snake got away! If you ever want to hear more snake stories, just ask me.

This is a picture of the machine gunner in dad's squad skinning a snake. The guy made a hat-band out of it and wore it on his "boonie" hat.

A couple of pictures of dead enemy soldiers. Dad took them with his own camera. The film was processed in Hawaii. Censors never allowed the printing of pictures of dead bodies and the film labs normally "blacked out" the negative to keep the pictures from being processed at a later date. Somehow, two of his negatives never got "blacked out" and dad found them years later and made prints. He said he took many such pictures but these two were the only negatives that made it past the censors.

Both pictures were taken of victims of his squad's ambush patrols.

The first one (an NVA soldier) was shot in the face at close range and the back of his head was pretty well blown off. The M-16 bullet hole can be seen in it's left cheek. The second picture is a dead Viet Cong, laying across a rice paddy dike, head in the water. His short pants were pulled down because no one could find a bullet hole on the body and everyone became a little curious as to how he died. When his pants were removed, a bullet hole was found on the right butt-cheek! Apparently the bullet had ranged upward into the body and struck something important, thus causing death.

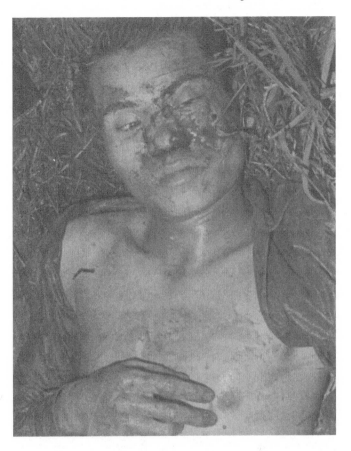

Richard Wright

A slightly out-of-focus picture of dad flashing a "peace" sign. As usual, up to his hips in mud and water.

Glossary Of Terminology

ARVN- Army Republic Viet Nam- generally used to refer to South Vietnamese soldiers. They were American allies during the war.

ARTY- artillery- one hundred-five millimeter howitzers were the most common. Usually grouped into units of about five weapons. They were stationed in the little base camps we worked out of. Arty shot both high-explosive rounds to help the infantry dislodge the enemy from their positions and illumination rounds to enable us to see at night when we "blew" ambushes.

BATTALION - a battalion consisted of four infantry companies (see company) and a Headquarters Company (H,Q.). the headquarters company stayed at the base camp and provided all the resources necessary to run the battalion. It included things like transportation, supply, communications, intelligence and much more. The HQ company is by far the largest company in a battalion. The cooks, the clerks, etc. were all attached to HQ company.

BOOBY-TRAP - hidden explosive device. They were usually no more complicated than a fragmentation grenade tied to a little stake next to the trail and camouflaged with leaves. A piece of string was then attached to the cotter pin of the grenade and strung across the trail, being anchored at the other end on another little stake or bush. The string was usually strung about ankle high and was next to impossible to see, as dirt being rubbed on the string would render it practically invisible. Other things were frequently used as booby-traps as well. Large "dud" artillery rounds were often rearmed by the VC/NVA and buried in the ground, rigged to explode when stepped on. Another trick they often used was to place an armed mortar round in the foliage about head high to an average G.I. We would then bump them with our heads and they would explode, tearing a man's head off. Booby-traps were like a plague in Viet Nam. They cost us a lot of casualties.

CLAYMORE-a concave shaped explosive device about six inches high and about ten inches wide, filled with C-4 explosive compound and hundreds of little steel pellets. Very deadly. It had little fold-up metal "legs" on the bottom to allow it to be stuck in the ground and pointed in any desired direction. It is a shaped-charge device, meaning that most of the blast power is focused in a single direction to maximize the effect of the explosion. The claymore was electrically detonated by means of an electrical wire with a blasting cap on one end and a battery-operated electric "trigger" device at the other end. G.I.'s called the triggering device a "clacker" due to the clacking noise it made when the "trigger" was pressed.

COBRA- a helicopter that was designed strictly as a weapons platform. It was much thinner in width and more maneuverable than a "huey". This chopper had a much more sleek profile. It's armament varied, but it usually had rocket "pods" on either side and a "chin turret" with some kind of automatic belt-fed weapon such as a three-barreled twenty millimeter cannon.

COLUMN-for the purposes of this book it would be defined as a group of soldiers walking single-file, one behind the next. A normal arrangement for soldiers when patrolling through the jungle or, for that matter, walking down a path or road.

COMPANY - an infantry company consists of three rifle platoons and one weapons platoon. The infantry platoons remain in the "field" most of the time. The weapons platoon usually stayed at the base camp. They served the eighty-one millimeter mortar (see mortar).

C.C. Ship- a helicopter that the battalion commander used. It would fly over head wherever trouble spots developed. The battalion commander could then direct the battle from above and be close enough to make command decisions. Other occupants in the chopper would be several RTO's to communicate with whomever the commander wanted. Also on board would be fire control officers to assist with artillery fire and things of that nature.

EAGLE FLIGHTS - also C.A.'s, or combat assault's (also see LZ) - for most of my tour, an eagle flight consisted of four choppers carrying a single platoon of infantry to a location determined by military intelligence to be occupied by the enemy. I did close to two hundred such combat insertions while in Viet Nam. Thank God military intelligence was usually wrong.

During my first five weeks in Viet Nam, I served in the Mobile Riverene Force. We worked in company sized groups. During that period and again in April 1970 we would be lifted two platoons at a time using eight choppers. The 9th Division was extremely "air mobile" and had a lot of helicopters at their disposal.

F-4 - generic name Army guy's used when referring to jets. I believe most of the jets were F-4's, but I'm sure others were used as well. For sure, there was at least one other type that were referred to as "sandies". they had straight wings as opposed to the rear-ward slant of the F-4's. they were a welcome sight when we hit enemy concentrations. Their loads of bombs or napalm was a life-saver for the lowly infantryman.

GUNSHIP- a basic "huey"helicopter that was convert-ed to a weapons platform. It usually had a pair of forward facing machine guns mounted on each side. It also had a "pod" holding rockets mounted on each side. These weap-ons were controlled by the pilots that operated the chopper. There were no door gunners on a gunship.

HUEY- nickname for the standard Bell Company heli-copter, designated the UH-1. The UH became pronounced as huey by the military. In it's most basic form it was called a "slick" (see slick).

HOWITZER- an artillery piece - the ones I saw were one hundred five millimeter's in bore diameter. They fired high-explosive rounds and illumination rounds in support of infantry operations - (see arty).

LAW- light anti-tank weapon- a bazooka like device that fired a sixty-six millimeter rocket full of high explo-sives. It was a "shaped" charge which means that the explo-sive force tended to be directionally focused as opposed to just blowing up in all directions like a grenade.

LOCH- pronounced "loach"- a small helicopter used primarily for observation purposes like spotting enemy locations for the heavily armed helicopter gun ships. Loch's were unarmed except for the personal fire arms the two man crew carried. They were easily identifiable due to their small size and the big plastic "bubble" front on it.'

"LUM"-illumination-flares configured to be shot out of mortars or howitzers. The flares had little parachutes attached to them and would pop open overhead to illuminate the area below it with an eerie greenish hue.

L.Z. - any place designated as a landing area for helicopters. Usual reference in this text was just a field or rice paddy large enough to land four helicopters (one platoon of G.I's) at the same time. The choppers would come in with the door gunners shooting, touch down for the briefest time possible to let the infantrymen scurry out, then lift off and get away as fast as possible.

M-16 - basic rifle used by the American soldier. It was introduced during the Viet Nam war. Initially their were a few problems with the rifle but the problems were soon solved. It was a very reliable weapon and has been the weapon of choice for the United States and many of it's allies for the past forty years. Don't believe the B.S. stories that are told about it's unreliability. It saved my life many a time.

The weapon had a twenty inch barrel. It has both full automatic and single shot capabilities. A twenty round magazine was standard during the Viet Nam war, but has since been superseded by a thirty round magazine.

M-79 - a single-shot weapon that fired a forty millimeter high-explosive round that was about as powerful as a hand grenade. It "broke open" like a single shot shotgun to be reloaded and, like a shotgun, the empty "shell" had to be extracted. It's chief advantages were it's accuracy and it's range. It could pretty accurately hit a six foot by six foot target at three hundred yards. The average hand thrown grenade could only be thrown about thirty yards or so. The M-79 was a valued weapon in a fire fight.

MAD MINUTE - everybody shoots to their immediate front for a brief minute. We did it just to see if we would "scare up" anything. It was generally only done the first thing in the morning after a night in the jungle when we had experienced trouble during the night.

MAGAZINE - the detachable twenty round device used to feed bullets into an M-16. We generally only loaded eighteen rounds per magazine to relieve stress on the internal spring that pushed up on the bullets to help feed them into the rifle. The basic "load" for a G.I. was supposed to be seven magazines. Everybody, and I mean everybody, carried a minimum of fifteen magazines. Often many of us carried as many as twenty-two on us when in the "bush".

MG- machine gun- M-60- a belt- fed fully automatic weapon weighing about twenty pounds. It was capable of sustained bursts of fire with out overheating too badly.

NAPALM - diesel, kerosene or gasoline mixed with some kind of "gelling" agent to make the fire stick to whatever it splashes onto. Very nasty stuff! Napalm was dropped by jets in large canisters. I don't know how much napalm was in one of those canisters, but I bet it was a hundred gallons or so. If a jet was armed with napalm it had two of those canisters, one under each wing. I never saw a "back-pack" type of flame thrower used in combat, only in training. They used the same basic mixture I think, as did the "Zippo's".

NDP - night defensive position - used by larger groups of soldiers usually, like a company sized unit. An NDP was used when staying over night in jungle that was too thick to move around in after dark. They were not considered ambush locations. An ambush location was considered an offensive position. NDP's were defensive positions.

NIPPAPALM - a plant that grew in profusion all over the swamps and jungle areas that I worked in. it had a single stalk that grew about fifteen or twenty feet high. On each stalk were row after row of leaves about a foot long that grew horizontally off the stalk. This plant can be seen in the pictures in this book. I think it just grew in the Southern areas of South Viet Nam, generally around the Mekong River.

PARACHUTE FLARE - a large flare with a parachute attached to it. Both mortars and artillery shot them. The artillery flares were larger, but both were adequate for the job of illuminating the area around us when "blowing" an ambush or needing to see at night for any other reason. They gave off a rather eerie green light. The sky in Viet Nam was full of these every night as much of the VC/NVA's activities were conducted in darkness. In fact, my experience in war would indicate that most of the trouble happened at night.

PLAIN OF REEDS - an uninhabited waste land that lay somewhat West of Saigon and extended westward to the Cambodian border. As Saigon was the political "prize" of the Viet Nam war, enemy troops used this region extensively to infiltrate closer to the Saigon area. The area was a vast expanse of unused rice paddies interspersed with small patches of jungle. These small patches of jungle were once the sites of small farm communities or "plantation" grounds long abandoned. It was criss-crossed with old hand dug canals. The edges of the canals were sometimes overgrown with jungle or more often overgrown with thick scrubby brush. The abandoned rice paddies were full of water year 'round and crotch high reeds grew in profusion in them.

Just across the Cambodian border lay huge VC/NVA base camps with supplies, rest areas, and training facilities. These area were off-limits to American G.I.'s and their allies until May of 1970, when we briefly invaded Cambodia to destroy the huge stockpiles of weaponry and disrupt the enemy supply lines.

PLATOON- basic army unit. My platoon in Viet Nam consisted of a five man CP group consisting of a lieutenant, also referred to as platoon leader- a platoon sergeant- a medic- and two RTO's, who carried radios. One of them usually communicated with the squads, the other usually had his radio frequency on a different band-width to communicate with higher up's.

The platoon also had two squads. Each squad had a squad leader- an RTO to carry a radio- a machine gunner to man the M-60 machine gun- an assistant machine gunner who's primary function was to carry an extra three hundred to four hundred rounds of ammo for the MG- and an M-79 man to carry the shotgun like grenade launcher- that's five people.

If I had an extra man I usually assigned him to be a second assistant to the machine gunner, and he would also carry three or four hundred rounds of MG ammo.

If I had two extra men, the second man carried a second M-79 grenade launcher.

In the rare event that I had three extra men, somebody would just be assigned as a rifleman. He got to carry extra equipment like a claymore mine and/or a hundred foot rope.

Eight men was about the best we could ever hope for.

The allocated strength of a platoon was three squads of twelve men each and a five man CP group. Perhaps this description will assist in helping to understand how critically short-handed and under strength we really were.

RECON BY FIRE - reconnaissance by fire - a euphemism for shooting up anything or any place that looked the least bit suspicious. Shooting into a specific area just to see what might happen. For example, if we thought an enemy soldier might be lying in hiding in a nearby clump of brush everybody nearby would pour fire into the clump of brush before going into it to see for sure. A "better safe than sorry" policy.

REGIMENT - also BRIGADE - generally consisted of three or four battalions.

RPG - rocket propelled grenade - don't let the name fool you. This was a single shot "bazooka" type weapon that fired a rocket about a foot long. It's armor piercing round was capable of taking out a tank! The RPG also fired a "bee-hive" round that G.I.'s hated. This round contained thousand's of little steel "darts" that flew through the air at high speed. They were called "bee-hive" rounds because of the buzzing sound that the little darts (fleschettes) made when they flew over our head's. The darts were capable of literally "pinning" a man to a tree. Very deadly. The "bee-hive" round was a very potent psychological weapon.

RTO- radio-telephone-operator. Basic instrument of communication. It weighed about fifteen pounds and was carried on a man's back. An FM radio. The hand-set, or "horn", looked like an old telephone hand-set.

SALVO- all of the guns in an artillery unit (usually five) firing a round more or less at the same time. In the Navy, it's called a "broadside".

SKIRMISH LINE- any number of soldiers aligned "shoulder-to-shoulder", usually about five yards apart. A basic strategy of combat when directly attacking. This maneuver made the individual soldier extremely vulnerable to enemy fire, particularly automatic weapons fire. However, it maximized a group of soldier's abilities to deliver "recon" or "suppressive" fire. Each man could fire directly to his front without worrying about shooting one of his fellow soldiers.

SLICK- a helicopter used for ferrying troops. It was stripped down for speed. Even the doors were taken off. The inner compartment would accommodate about six people. It's only armament was a door gunner on each side with an M-60 machine gun.

SPIDER-HOLE - a small one-man hole, usually no more than eighteen inches in diameter and deep enough for a small man to squat down in and hide. They were very hard to spot as the VC/NVA usually had a camouflaged wooden cover to put over the hole to conceal it.

STARLIGHT SCOPE - a night vision device. As an over-simplification, it was basically a large rifle telescope. The device was capable of amplifying the ambient light from the moon or the stars to enable us to see at night. It was battery powered. Each infantry squad was issued one. They were useless in the jungle but extremely valuable out in the open rice paddies. Doing night ambush patrols without them would have been very difficult.

SUPPRESSIVE FIRE-a high volume of fire being put out by any number of soldiers, be it one man or an entire company of soldiers. It's purpose is to make the enemy soldiers "keep their heads down" and not be able to return fire. Theoretically, this would enable other groups of soldiers to maneuver more freely. Liberal use of suppressive fire allowed soldiers movement, whether it be to attack an enemy position from a flank, evacuate casualties, or just move back a little to a more protected position. A basic strategy of combat.

"TANGO" BOAT- a Navy boat used to ferry troops in. it was actually designed for use as an assault boat. Assault troops were loaded into them and carried to shore when the first "waves" of soldiers "hit" the beach. They were about large enough to carry one tank in if necessary. They had an open topped troop compartment in the front and a little "tower" in the rear where the Navy guys stood to steer the boat. See picture in early chapters of book.

VC/NVA - Viet Cong/ North Vietnamese Army - two foes were fought in Viet Nam. In the NVA were soldiers recruited or drafted into North Viet Nam's regular Army and sent to South Viet Nam to fight. They fought both as regular Army units and as replacements into the ranks of the Viet Cong.

The Viet Cong, on the other hand, were South Vietnamese with Communist Party loyalties. Some Viet Cong were organized into regular army type units and engaged in more traditional type large unit combat operations. Other groups of Viet Cong were "guerillas" who farmed by day and laid ambush's and Booby-traps by night. Some Viet-Cong units were provided with military uniforms and some were not. The "guerillas" never had uniforms.

At any rate, in the areas that I worked in, almost all enemy soldiers shed their uniforms and wore civilian clothes to better blend in with the civilian population, thus making them hard to identify until they started shooting at you.

All of these little guys were formidable foes! Perhaps the VC "guerilla" was the worst of the bunch. He was fighting in his own back yard so he knew his immediate terrain very well. That is a decided advantage in jungle warfare. The "guerilla" was also highly politically motivated.

The NVA had a little more fire power, but the Viet Cong had more maneuverability. The Viet Cong were masters of both ambush and the placing of booby-traps. Their "hit and run" tactics were very frustrating!

50966649R00128

Made in the USA
Lexington, KY
06 April 2016